PORT

Andrew Jefford

NEW YORK

Author's acknowledgements

THIS BOOK is written by a port enthusiast. Enthusiasm is at best a partial substitute for professional knowledge and experience, though, and I am very grateful to the many professionals who have generously given me their time and allowed me to profit from their knowledge and experience. In particular I would like to thank Michael Symington of Dow's Port for reading the manuscript and suggesting a number of valuable corrections and emendations; Cristiano van Zeller of Quinta do Noval for answering so many questions so courteously; and Dirk van der Niepoort of Niepoort for generous help of every sort from Portugal. Any remaining errors are my sole responsibility.

First published in USA 1988
by Exeter Books

Distributed by Bookthrift

Exeter is a trademark of Bookthrift Marketing Inc.

Bookthrift is a registered trademark of
Bookthrift Marketing Inc.
New York, New York

Devised and produced by Templar Publishing Ltd,
107 High Street, Dorking, Surrey, RH4 1QA

Copyright © 1988 by Templar Publishing

Editor: Mary Lambert
House editor: Amanda Wood
Designer: Hector B.
Typesetting: Servis Filmsetting Ltd, Manchester
Colour separations by J Film Process Ltd, London
Printed and bound by Motta, Milan, Italy

ISBN 0-671-10032

Contents

PORTO
RAMOS-PINTO

Foreword

The Portuguese say "Port is the cure for all ills save death". In Britain, not infrequently, those feeling like death, forgetting their pre-prandial intake and those magnums now lying empty by the back door, blame all their ills on their last drink – one relatively small glass of port. With such a handicap the pleasures of port need constant emphasis and I like to think that, in writing this foreword to an excellent book by a young author, I am continuing the good work I started in the 1950s when port was in the doldrums.

During the war, by a stroke of good fortune, I had met Claire Bergqvist, neé Feuerheerd, the family who owned Quinta La Rosa at Pinhão. Thus in Peter Dominic – a private firm with only ten branches in 1955 – we could boast of 'Our Resident Douro Correspondent' when I created and edited *Wine Mine*, my firm's combined price list and magazine from 1959 to 1974.

Only since 1969 has there been a succession of good up-to-date guides to port, from Sarah Bradford (1969), George Robertson (1978) and Ben Howkins (1982) – all three contributors to *Wine Mine*. These labours of love are now generously commended by Andrew Jefford in this, his worthy successor.

He begins rightly with the great river of gold, life blood of the port trade and now, through its thirteen dams, a generator of half the nation's electricity. Soon it will become a navigable waterway for vessels exporting Spanish and Portuguese iron ore extracted from the mountains. Tourism will benefit too. Next he tells the fascinating story of how rough red table wine, 'Red Portugal', when fortified with local brandy became a sweet, unsurpassed dessert wine if left to improve in cask for up to twenty years. And, once there was a cork and a glass bottle shaped so that it would lie down, how a much fuller sort of port, called 'Vintage', would emerge from that bottle after much the same duration.

Compared to the old days of little more than Vintage, Tawny and Ruby, the choice of port available today has been greatly widened, mainly to provide full-bodied wines ready to drink without decanting at club and business functions. Amounting to less than 5% of all port production, true Vintage Port – bottled after two years only if the shipper has declared a vintage – is magnificent, but only those who ride to hounds twice a week or jog to work daily should make a habit of it. Regular drinkers keep to Tawny, a lighter, any-weather drink; superb at '10 years old', the label '20 years old' indicates the quintessence.

No wine is better regulated than port. Its name (*Porto* in America) is protected. The Douro was the first of the world's wine regions to be demarcated; in 1758 to 1761, at least a century before any others. The *Casa do Douro* representing the growers keeps a detailed register of 84,000 vineyards. The shippers have their own Association, while the Port Wine Institute is the co-ordinating Government body, whose *selo de garantia* is fixed on each bottle between cork and capsule.

Shipping their brands worldwide nowadays, business must be booming for Port shippers. In the Douro valley mechanical monsters, high above the river, furrow new vineyards along precipitous slopes. Machines pick the grapes and autovinificators make the wine. Yet still the shippers are not sure whether machines make a better port than the human foot. In the Douro, old ways die hard.

In a famous Champagne court case, André Simon declared, "I am absolutely full of my subject" Those who read this thoroughly informative guide should undoubtedly achieve a similar distinction, and 'Pass the Port' too if taking Exams in the Trade.

Anthony Hogg.

Port in Perspective

". . . he pours a radiant nectar . . . that fills the whole room with the fragrance of Southern grapes . . ."
Charles Dickens
(Bleak House)

What does the word 'port' suggest to you? Several things, no doubt; but in this context, your thoughts will turn to a glass of red dessert wine. You may happen to know that this wine contains brandy: it has been fortified, to use the not-very-technical term. In the simplest sense, that is what port – in a glass – is: a red wine that has had brandy added to it, and tastes more or less sweet. Exactly why this is so is explained later in the book.

But 'port' suggests much more than this plain definition. Consider the luxurious sound of the word, expressive of comfort, fireside warmth, upholstered ease. Add an adjectival ending and you have 'portly', meaning stout or corpulent: it might almost be the condition of having enjoyed too much port for too long. Here two images spring to mind: one of a monocled colonel in a London club, spluttering over an inaccuracy in a fellow officer's *Times* obituary; another of a gouty English squire, laid up in bed in his damp shire manor house, unable to join the Boxing Day hunt, and making his housekeeper's life a misery as a consequence. These are the old clichés of port, fast disappearing today.

To those involved with the sea, the word 'port' holds other associations: larboard, the left side, and then the harbour or haven reached at journey's end. As it happens, these are more appropriate images for our glass of wine, a wine that is almost entirely the creation of its shippers. Port takes its name from Oporto, the northern Portuguese port from which all true port wine had, until 1986, to be shipped. The Portuguese name for this, their second biggest city, is simply Porto; *o porto* in Portuguese means 'the port'. A glass of Porto anywhere in the world, or Port in Britain, will mean only one thing: fortified wine from the demarcated area surrounding the upper reaches of the Portuguese Douro, the river

which issues into the Atlantic a little downstream of Oporto, at Foz. Part One of this book will describe how port may be further defined.

Before turning to these details, though, it would be useful to learn a little more of the background to this rich subject. What of the Alto Douro (High Douro) region and the Rio Douro itself – the river of gold? What of the people who live there, grow the grapes and make the wine?

The Douro begins its life as the Duero, high in the Spanish Sierra de Urbión. A short helicopter hop north from the source would take you over the peaks and into Rioja country, from where much of Spain's best table wine comes. The Spanish name 'Duero' also means 'of gold'. Some say tiny deposits of this metal are to be found in the river bed, while others claim the name is a misnomer, deriving from the milky amber colour of the mud-charged river after the winter rains. Three quarters of its 900 km (560 mile) course is, in fact, in Spain, as it traces a leisurely westward path across the plains of Old Castile. Here, again, the river is linked with fine wine, for both the Ribera del Duero and Rueda *Denominación de Origen* areas either surround or border the Douro. Vega Sicilia, Spain's single answer to France's Château Latour and Australia's Grange Hermitage, is produced in the Ribera del Duero, about 40 km (25 miles) east of Valladolid. Even before the Portuguese border is reached, the Duero/ Douro begins to look as important a wine river as the Rhine, the Rhône or the Loire. By the time it reaches Oporto, the case is convincingly argued.

The Duero arrives at the Portuguese border about 10 km (six miles) north of Miranda do Douro, and the river then forms a natural border between the two countries for about 100 km (70 miles), as far as Barca de Alva. This was once a particularly violent stretch of water, marked by many gorges and rapids: the high plains ended and the Douro set about carving its path to the sea with fervour. In recent years dams and power stations have been built, tapping some of this energy and calming its course. At Barca de Alva the river continues westwards to the sea, while the border continues southwards, dividing Portugal's Beira Alta from Spain's Extremadura.

The demarcated area (or *Região Demarcada* – remember that in Portuguese '-*ão*' is pronounced as a nasalized 'on': the words will suddenly seem more familiar to you) for port production is shown on the map on page 13. The vineyards fan out irregularly on both sides of the river. The area covers just under 243,000 hectares (1,000 sq miles), of which only ten per cent is currently under vines. The port wine-growing area, incidentally, was the first such area anywhere in the world to be demarcated: the survey was begun in 1758 and completed in 1761. The boundaries have changed substantially since then, but not the search for quality that self-imposed restrictions of this sort represent.

THE SCALE and grandeur of the Douro are both emphasized by long evening shadows on the flanks of the hills.

An island of schist

The Upper Douro is an awe-inspiring place. Geologically speaking, the port wine-producing part of this region is an island of schist in a sea of granite. The schist, as we shall see later, provides perfect growing conditions for vines. The result is a landscape of high drama: hills and valleys as fertile and green in summer as they are rugged and bare in winter; steep slopes whose relief is rendered with cartographic accuracy by line on line of rippling terraces. The river and its tributaries have cut deeply into the rock, and twist towards the sea with an energy that seems to belong to an earlier geological era than our own. The wildlife reflects this boldness in the land: golden eagles, wolves, martens and lynx are still to be found in the remoter parts of the Douro. The climate is harsh in both winter and summer, as the temperature regularly sinks below freezing point in January and February, before rising to over 40°C (104°F) in July and August. Spring and early summer are lovely, as the rains bring out a profusion of brightly coloured and scented flowers, such as honeysuckle, mimosa, cornflower, iris and jonquil. Autumn is beautiful too, thanks to the large number of grape varieties grown in the region: in late September and October the leaves of each variety turn a different shade of yellow, red, russet or brown.

Most of the port production area lies in the province of Trás-os-Montes e Alto Douro. 'Trás-os-Montes' means 'beyond the mountains', and this gives some idea of the remoteness of the region where until recently, the little railway that followed the course of the river provided the only alternative to horse or mule transport. As is natural, the character of the people reflects the environment in which they and their ancestors have made their lives. The farmers and villagers of the Alto Douro are stubborn and uncompromising to a near-granitic degree. To outsiders, they can seem as hostile and unwelcoming as the coldest winter snap, while to those who have gained their confidence and trust, they are unceasingly warm and hospitable. Above all they are traditionalists, conservative in every aspect of their being. Time has no more softened their edges than it has smoothed the surface of the Alto Douro.

Farmers will grow and then sell their grapes (in the old days it would have been their wines) to the same shipper or shippers, year after year: the original agreement was arrived at by handshake

Portugal and the Demarcated Douro Region

*S*TAKES OF slate are hammered into rocky soil to support the Douro's hardy vines.

KEY TO MAJOR QUINTAS
1 Casa dos Alembiques
2 Quinta do Côtto
3 Quinta da Boa Vista
4 Quinta la Rosa
5 Quinta do Panascal
6 Quinta da Côrte
7 Quinta da Foz
8 Quinta da Eira Velha
9 Quinta do Junco
10 Quinta das Carvalhas
11 Quinta do Bom-Retiro
12 Quinta do Noval
13 Quinta do Bomfim
14 Quinta da Roêda
15 Quinta dos Malvedos
16 Quinta do Roriz
17 Quinta da Tua
18 Quinta de Vargellas
19 Quinta do Vesúvio
20 Quinta do Vale de Meão

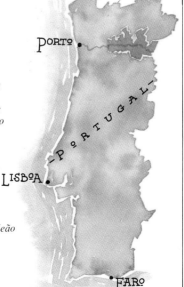

perhaps a 100 years earlier, and neither party has questioned the arrangement since. Every aspect of the vineyard year has its rituals, from the arrival of the hard-drinking *podadores* (pruners) in the late autumn to the departure of the *roga* (a grape-picking team of men, women and children from the same mountain village) after the harvest, when the *ramo*, a strangely decorated cane, is handed to the lady of the house to the accompaniment of a traditional verse.

A crucial factor in the development of port over the last four or five centuries has been the comparatively high population density of the areas bordering the rural Alto Douro (itself sparsely populated). The men and women from villages to the north, south and west of the wine-growing centre have traditionally provided the manpower needed for even routine jobs on the wine-farms. It was this resource that meant that the necessary terraces could be built, soil prepared, grapes picked and then trodden by foot, and wine transported by the ancient *barcos rabelos* downriver to Oporto. The departure of this manpower following industrialization to the cities, in emigration to Brazil at the turn of the century, and

THE GRAPE-PORTERS or borracheiros *labour on the terraces. Each basket contains a small man's weight in grapes. Mechanization of this task is impossible.*

to France and Belgium after World War II, has posed grave problems for the shippers. These have been intensified by the enormous difficulties that lie in the path of vineyard mechanization in a remote and mountainous region. Part Two of the book will examine the question of port production past and present in considerable detail.

What, though, of the substance itself – that glass of red dessert wine with which we began?

Crusaders, doctors and dons

Port's past does not belong exclusively to English colonels and squires – far from it. Most port shipped from Oporto has always been enjoyed by ordinary people who like good, reasonably priced, wine. Part Three of the book will discuss the enjoyment of port from this standpoint. One important historical change has taken place, though, in that the wine our early 18th century ancestors and their forebears would have enjoyed would not nowadays be described as port, but as Douro table wine. It was a big, harsh, fierce drink, familiarly known as 'blackstrap': this was what Dr Johnson had in mind when he said that "Claret is the liquor for boys; port for men". It was very dry to taste and unfortified (though a bucket or so of brandy may have been thrown into each cask by the shipper to 'help it travel'), and it was generally purchased from the wood in pint jugs. Tennyson was later to record this practice, in *Will Waterproof's Lyrical Monologue* (*Made at The Cock*):

O plump head-waiter at The Cock,
   To which I most resort.
How goes the time? 'Tis five o'clock.
   Go fetch a pint of port.

In earlier times still, the wine was thinner and lighter, rather like the red *vinho verde* that today's tourists, travelling in the north of Portugal, will know well. This would have been the wine that the first English would have sustained themselves with: crusaders called upon to expel the Moors from Lisbon (which they did in 1147) and the south of Portugal. It probably did not matter much to them what the wine tasted like, so long as it contained alcohol: they travelled with much the same reputation as English football fans enjoy today. "Plunderers, drunkards and rapists, men not seasoned with the honey of piety," wrote a contemporary chronicler; the contrast with the civilized Muslim Moors was striking. Civilization was no defence, though: by 1249 the last Moorish stronghold, Faro, had fallen. The borders of Portugal established then were much as they are today.

This light red wine was what was meant by 'red Portugal' until the mid- to late 17th century. Like many light red wines it did not travel well or mature in any way, and it was not popular. The British Navy bought it as a 'beverage wine' for their sailors, and in the state papers for 1662 one Consul Maynard is noted as having "sent his bills for beverage Wines for the Navy. Asks an order to dispose of the remaining wines which are spoiling."

By the 19th century, though, port had evolved into the sweet, fortified wine we recognize today. It was enjoyed by all. George Saintsbury, in his

*O*PORTO, VIEWED *with an early 20th century engraver's tranquillity (above). A* barco rabelo, *its adventurous descent of the Douro completed, is rowed to berth.*

*B*ARE-FOOTED *and straight-backed, Portuguese women (left) have always carried loads on their heads – perhaps a Moorish legacy – and still do so today. These grape-pickers are at work at Graham's Quinta dos Malvedos, circa 1900.*

famous *Notes on a Cellar Book*, says that at Oxford and Cambridge port was "The milk of donhood", and David Cecil (in *Lord M.*) describes Lord Chancellor Brougham's defence of the Reform Bill under its influence: "His speech culminated in a peroration in which, falling on his knees and with outstretched hands, he implored the Peers not to throw out the Bill. Unluckily, in order to stimulate his eloquence, he had during his speech drunk a whole bottle of mulled port, with the result that once on his knees he found he was unable to get up until assisted to do so by his embarrassed colleagues." Middle-class Victorian households kept decanters of both sherry and port, and when the levels grew low the two were mixed together to form a peculiar blend known as 'matrimony'; while Surtees' Mr Jorrocks, Cockney grocer and precursor of Mr Pickwick, was also devoted to port, which he classed as "... a good fruity wine; with a grip o' the gob that leaves a mark on the side o' the glass ...". Britain took most of the port exported, though what had been a 90 per cent share in the 1840s had dropped to around 60 per cent by the turn of the century.

All began well for the port shippers in the 20th century. The great vine pest phylloxera (see page 40) had been overcome; vintage port appreciation was at its zenith; world port markets were expanding. Higher taxes in Britain on spirits meant that port-and-lemon replaced gin as the lady's favoured pub drink, and this alone accounted for huge volume sales (80 per cent of all port imported into Britain was soon to be consumed in pubs). Storm clouds, though, were gathering.

By the end of the 1920s cocktail parties were all the rage amongst the rich, while the middle classes had taken to giving sherry parties. 'Empire ports' exported from Australia and other countries benefited from favourable rates of duty. The circumstances of life were changing: people led increasingly sedentary lives, and the enormous meals of Georgian and Victorian times began to seem passé. Dinners shrank to a mere three or four courses, and diners no longer instinctively reached for the port decanter at the end of them. Nevertheless, after some difficult times in the early 1930s, trade remained reasonably buoyant until war broke out.

The port trade stagnated during World War II. Portugal remained neutral, but strict quotas were applied to shipments of this luxury item, and these remained in force until 1949. When the quotas were lifted, somehow people did not seem interested in port any more. It was felt to be part of the past. New

*P*ORT IS *widely believed to provoke gout. This erroneous belief has existed for centuries, and was common at the time that this cartoon was published in* 1799. *In fact, excess uric acid in the blood is the cause of this mainly hereditary complaint.*

competition, in the form of 'British wine' (made from imported grape juice concentrate) and sweet Cyprus sherry, captured the previously all-important British market for inexpensive dessert wine. Some hard thinking had to be done in the port lodges in Vila Nova de Gaia.

A major reason for the crisis experienced by the port trade at this time had been the failure – one shipper excepted – to foresee future buying trends. Port shippers are as conservative in their outlook as Douro farmers, which may be why they have got on together, despite temporary altercations, for so long. Port had traditionally been sold in bulk to English merchants by 'mark' (a sign branded onto a cask to signify the wine's style and quality), and these merchants had then bottled it and labelled it themselves. Advertising and building brand names was considered vulgar and in bad taste. The one shipper who broke ranks in the 1920s and did these things – Sandeman – was sneered at, and its product dismissed as 'grocer's port'. Today, as a direct consequence of its foresight, Sandeman is the biggest single British shipper.

Retrenchment and rationalization took place within the trade. Many old names disappeared, and many more reorganized themselves into groups. A number of shippers were taken over by leading British and international drinks companies. Brands

RAMOS-PINTO'S poster artist had no truck with the gout myth (left). "To health!" ("A saúde!" in Portuguese) toasts this slim, elegant port-drinker.

THE FAMOUS shadowy Don (below) takes a secretive glass of tawny. Sandeman's advertising lead over its rivals has helped make it the biggest single British shipper.

began to appear. Most importantly of all, the image of port began to change: the colonels and squires faded into history, and port became a wine again, not just an outdated tradition.

In the face of fashion

It is as a wine – a fortified wine of quality, unique in its geographical origins and methods of manufacture – that port faces the future. The confidence of the port trade has been restored. Instead of further retrenchment, a new independent shipper began exporting in 1981: Churchill Graham. New plantings of vines, often in areas abandoned since the phylloxera scourge, are taking place every year in the best parts of the Alto Douro. The market for port is now thoroughly international, with white and tawny ports selling well in warmer countries, and ruby ports, fine tawnies and the vintage 'family' of ports maintaining or increasing sales in colder climates. The end of the century is expected by the shippers to be as good for business as was the beginning.

There is, though, something surprising in all this. The great majority of the wine world's success stories in recent years have been with dry or medium dry white wines, often slightly sparkling, and generally low in alcohol. White *vinho verde* is a good example of this internationally favoured style. The key words for the wine consumer in the last quarter of the 20th century seem to be 'light' and 'crisp'. How is it that port, with its unctuous texture, its sweetness and low acidity levels, and its 20 or so degrees of alcohol – with the wind of fashion blowing full against it – continues both to command an enthusiastic following, and win new converts?

We have already touched on part of the answer: the fact that port is unique, that no other fortified wine is quite like it. There is a magic rightness about port – as about Champagne, say, or Cognac – that defies analysis. It is indispensable. The rest of the answer lies in the way in which port is produced – as a fortified wine of the highest quality. Wine drinkers nowadays enjoy more choice, and exercise more discernment, than at any other time in history, and there seems certain to be an expanding market for quality wines of every sort in the decades to come. The regulations and traditions that govern port's production guarantee that it will always be a quality wine like no other, and at best one of the world's great wines: the perfect expression of the grapes, soils and climate of its splendid and savage upland.

PART ONE

What is Port?

"Claret is the liquor for boys; port for men . . ."
Doctor Johnson
(Boswell's Life of Johnson)

At the time of the crusaders, as we know from the Introduction, 'red Portugal' was a light, sharp wine, an 'eager' wine, rather like red *vinho verde*. By Doctor Johnson's day, 'red Portugal' had become 'port', grown in the Douro and shipped out of Oporto: a harsh, astringently dry wine that sorted the men from the boys. Today it is rich and sweet. Which is the true port?

'Red Portugal' would not qualify as port today, as it would have been produced outside the demarcated port area, probably in the Minho and perhaps in the lower Douro. Doctor Johnson's port, by contrast, might well qualify on a geographical basis. But at that time the secret of port had not been discovered, and the wines were fermented through until no sugar remained in them. They were still table wines.

True port, in the modern sense, began to be exported between 1700 and 1775, though it was not until 1850 or so that the consumer could expect any uniformity in port winemaking. The secret was not discovered overnight. Winemaking then was a haphazard business, and much that is taken for granted nowadays, like an understanding of the processes of fermentation, or the existence of bacteria in the air, was not known then. Many things could go wrong between grape and wine glass, and success and failure must both, at times, have seemed accidental.

The secret was not merely fortification of the young wine with brandy, but fortification at the right time: when the wine was still a fermenting must. The sweetness of port is natural. It is the sweetness of the grape when picked – the result of a long hot Douro summer. In fermentation, grape sugars are converted by the action of natural yeasts to alcohol. (Yeasts are tiny fungi that consume sugar, giving off equal quantities of carbon dioxide and alcohol.) The normal course of things is for the yeasts to continue to ferment until little or no sugar is left in the wine, as it has all been converted to alcohol and carbon dioxide (released into the atmosphere). This would give us Doctor Johnson's port. To produce modern port, 'full strength' brandy (77 per cent alcohol by volume: nearly twice as strong as most commercially available spirits – and in that state, undrinkable) is added to the wine halfway through fermentation. The alcohol stuns the yeasts, which cannot continue to operate in wines of above 16° or 17° of alcohol, and fermentation stops. The remaining grape sugar is not converted into alcohol, and the wine is consequently sweet to taste.

All port, whether ruby, tawny, vintage or white, is made in this way. The differences between these various types of port are the result of how they are treated after fermentation and fortification – white port excepted, of course, as it is made with white and not red grapes. These differences will be examined in detail in a few pages.

Port wine legislation

Before doing this, though, it will be useful to turn to the legal aspects of port wine production, and to examine the structure of the trade. It is often said that port is the most closely controlled of all the world's wines. This is true: legislation began early, and has been subject to constant modifications and refinements ever since. The centralization of the trade in the single entrepôt (export trade zone) of Vila Nova de Gaia, opposite Oporto, has made enforcement comparatively easy; so has the innate conservatism of both the Portuguese and British, who tend to see laws in a positive light: as traditions that work. Anathema to Italian winemakers!

The Douro, as mentioned in the Introduction, was the first of the world's wine-growing regions to be demarcated, between 1758 and 1761, and the impetus for this came from Sebastião de Carvalho, at that time Conde de Oeiras, and later Marquês de Pombal (1699–1782). This extraordinary man, born Sebastião José de Carvalho e Mello, dominated Portuguese national and political life for over 25 years, throughout the reign of King José I (1750–1777). He was a despotic reformer, whose aims were in the main as laudable as his methods were unscrupulous. Few economically important sectors of Portuguese life escaped his attentions, and the profitable British-dominated wine trade was certainly not one of them.

Since the Anglo–Portuguese 'favoured nation' treaty of 1654, British merchants in Portugal had enjoyed numerous trading privileges. The wine shippers among them had begun to abuse these of late, wanting the growers to produce a wine

> . . . to exceed the limits which nature had assigned to it, [so] that when drunk, it should feel like liquid fire in the stomach; that it should burn like inflamed gunpowder; that it should have the tint of ink; that it should be like the sugar of Brazil in sweetness, and like the spices of India in aromatic flavour. They began by recommending, by way of secret, that it was proper to dash it with brandy to give it strength; and with elderberries, or the rind of the ripe grape, to give it colour; and as the persons who used the prescription found the wines increase in price, and the English merchants still complaining of a want of strength, colour and maturity in the article supplied, the recipe was propagated till the wines became a mere confusion of mixtures.

So wrote the growers' agents in a joint letter to the shippers during 1754.

Pombal was familiar with the British. One of his early career successes had been seven years of astute diplomacy in London, and he quickly outmanoeuvred the complacent shippers. In 1756 he set up a National Board of Trade (Junta do Comércio), to limit the operating freedom of all foreign merchants in Portugal. On the 10th September of the same year, following an appeal by the wine growers who had been particularly shabbily treated that summer by the shippers, he established a wine monopoly: the Companhia Geral da Agricultura

THE MARQUÊS de Pombal, seen here with plans for the rebuilding of Lisbon after the 1755 earthquake. Pombal was responsible for the world's first demarcation of a wine-growing area: the *schistous parts of the Alto Douro, for port (1758–61).*

dos Vinhos do Alto Douro. In addition to delimiting the area (or 'Factory Zone') in which port wine could be made, he forbade adulteration of the wines with elderberry juice, and the fertilizing of the vines with manure (which led to overproduction), and gave to his company the exclusive right to distil the grape brandy which was added to the wines. The Companhia also controlled all grape prices, enjoyed a monopoly of the wine trade with Britain and Brazil, and was the only company allowed to supply wines to Oporto taverns. This last privilege caused an unexpected hiccup in Pombal's plans: as the growers were now paid a fair price for their wines, the cost to the tavern keepers and their drinking customers rose accordingly. This provoked the 'Tipplers' Riots' of 1757, which were repressed with characteristic brutality. Pombal suspected the British merchants of having had a hand in fomenting them, and he was probably right.

*T*HE DOM *Luis I Bridge
(built 1881–85), viewed
from the Vila Nova de Gala
side of the Douro (left).
Cars, lorries and buses can be
seen making the journey to
and from Oporto some 180 m
(591 ft) above the water.*

*W*ITH NO BRANDS *and
few shippers' names,
these two lists (below), from
1891 and 1886, show ports
sold on description alone.
Each would be matched by a
burnt shipper's mark on the
export pipe. The popularity of
vintage port can be gauged by
the range offered.*

The quality of the wine improved, though; within a few years it had improved beyond all measure. The Companhia was corrupt from top to bottom, but somehow its good intentions got the better of it. Important measures for the future were brought about at its instigation, such as opening the offshore ridge of the Douro and dredging the river mouth; clearing the rapids of the Cachão da Valeira of the huge granite slabs blocking the way upstream to the best vineyards of the Alto Douro; road-building; and the development of local oak forests to provide timber for cask-making. After Pombal's death in 1777, it gradually eased its monopolistic control of the trade.

The effectiveness of Pombal's legislation, and of his demarcation of the Factory Zone in particular, can be gauged by the fact that although revisions were made to it in 1788 and subsequently, no one has ever questioned its existence. Quite the opposite: its example has been widely followed the world over. The monopoly, by contrast, was dissolved in time, the Companhia becoming a shipper like any other in 1834. In 1838 some of its former powers were given back to it for a 20-year period; then in 1865 it again became a shipper trading on the same terms as everyone else. So things remained until the Companhia was taken over, after World War II, by

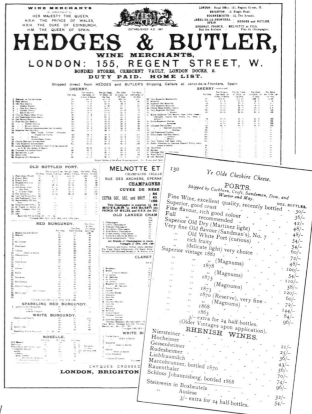

*T*HE *INSTITUTO do Vinho do Porto's* Selo de Garantia *(above) will be found on all authentic bottle-exported port (though not on authentic port exported in cask and bottled abroad).*

*O*PORTO'S ATLANTIC *climate (right) ensures that its grass is always green (it has twice London's annual rainfall), and its winters are warm enough for palms to flourish.*

the large Real Companhia Vinícola do Norte de Portugal, nationalized in 1975, and denationalized again in 1978. Its wines are now sold on English-speaking markets under the 'Royal Oporto Wine Company' name.

New legislation

In 1905 the port shippers, alarmed by the arrival in Britain (their biggest export market then) of cheap 'Empire ports' from Australia and elsewhere approached the Foreign Office to try and protect the name of port. Negotiations were lengthy, but in the Anglo–Portuguese Commercial Treaty Act of 1914 the government engaged "to recommend to Parliament to prohibit the importation of any wine or other liquor to which the description 'Port' or 'Madeira' is applied other than the produce of Portugal and of the island of Madeira respectively." (It took the shippers until 1968 to protect port's name – as 'Porto' – on the American market.) Meanwhile, major revisions had been made to the demarcated area in 1907 and 1908 under the guidance of prime minister João Franco.

By 1933 the Portuguese government had established a complete system of control over every stage

of port production. This was necessary as abuses had arisen during the boom years of the 1920s, when port had, briefly, provided quick profits for the unscrupulous. The system established then remains substantially unchanged today.

Three organizations oversee each stage of port production. The Casa do Douro, whose headquarters are at Peso da Régua, the capital of the port-producing region, is an association to which farmers and wine growers must belong. It oversees the initial stages of port production: vine selection and vineyard plantings, correct vinification (wine-making) procedures, the fortification of musts with brandy. It also acts as a broker on behalf of the government, buying up wines in times of plenty, storing them, and releasing them in poor years. The shippers' counterpart to this was originally the Grémio dos Exportadores do Vinho do Porto (the Port Wine Shippers' Association), and all port shippers had to belong. After the Portuguese 'Revolution of Flowers' in 1974, which put an end to the Salazar regime (in force since 1933), the Grémio was dissolved, and the Associação dos Exportadores do Vinho do Porto took its place. Membership became optional, and there was no longer a government representative on the board. The Associação is as important a body as its predecessor, however, acting on behalf of its members in all matters affecting the shippers' livelihood.

The third organization is the Instituto do Vinho do Porto – the Port Wine Institute. This is the coordinating government body to which the other two groups were originally subject, though again there has been a loosening of the rules since 1974. The Institute decrees what percentage of the Douro's wine may be turned into port each year, and what is the maximum and minimum price that should be paid by shippers to growers for their grapes or their wine. It also controls shipping rights: no shipper is allowed to export more than a third of the stock held at the beginning of that year. This law, known as the *lei de terço*, is designed to ensure that basic qualities of port are properly matured, and that those shipping port have a serious and responsible stockholding interest in the wine.

The Institute monitors the movement of port in, and shipments from, the port entrepôt of Vila Nova de Gaia (there is now also a smaller entrepôt at Régua), and tests and analyzes all blends of port. Bulk shipments are then given a Certificate of Origin, while bottled ports receive their Certificate of Origin together with the *selo de garantia* – the sober little black-and-white strip of paper that runs over the cork and under the capsule – from the Institute. Only after the award of the Certificate is the wine officially recognized as Port, or Porto.

The Inspectors of the Institute are allowed to enter any shippers' lodge at any time, if they are not happy with the conduct of the shipper, and demand information or an account of the questionable practice. They even have sentry boxes, positioned to delimit the *entreposto* of Vila Nova de Gaia.

A vineyard register

Before finishing with port officialdom, it is worth examining one particularly interesting aspect of the authorities' superintendence of production. Shortly after the Casa do Douro was created a survey of vineyards was undertaken, in 1937. In an area as remote and of such uneven relief as the Alto Douro, this was a heroic undertaking: little wonder that it took eight years to complete. More startling still is its intricacy. To anyone of a Linnaean turn of mind, the Register, as it is known, is a delight. It is also useful, as it governs the proportion of each vineyard's wine that can be made into port every year (the better the vineyard, the higher the proportion).

Each vineyard is given a number of points for 14 different features: altitude, productivity, nature of the land, locality, vine training system, grape varieties and quality, slope, aspect, density of vines, soil and degree of stoniness, age of vines, and available shelter. The points maxima for each category are different: locality is felt to be the most important positive factor, and up to 600 points can be awarded for this, while 50 points is the maximum available for an ideal density of vines. Some categories also carry penalty points: unfavourable altitude and high, but poorer quality produce can both lose a vineyard up to 900 points, and are the two most negative factors. All the plus and minus factors are then computed to give a points total, and this will put the vineyard into one of six alphabetically coded groups. Group A vineyards are those that have scored 1,200 or more points, and can make up to 700 litres (154 gal) of port every year per 1,000 vines; Group E vineyards are those that have scored between 401 and 600 points, and can make only 300 litres (66 gal) of port per 1,000 vines. Group F vineyards (201 to 400 points) have no authorization to make port, and will make table wines instead, as will the middle quality vineyards in addition to their port allowance. The Register (or *Cadastro* in Portu-

EVERY ONE of the Douro's crumpled patchwork of vineyards has been classified, and classified minutely, in the Casa do Douro's Register.

guese) has been updated since its inception for the classification of new vineyards and reassessment of those renovated. To appreciate the full measure of the task, it should be noted that in 1984 there were 83,841 properties in the region, worked by 29,619 wine farmers. Most of these are very small properties: about three-quarters of the farms produce five pipes of port or fewer a year (a 'pipe' or *pipa* is a port wine cask containing 550 litres/121 gal in the Douro, and 534 litres/117 gal for shipping purposes). Only two per cent of the farms are large properties which produce over 50 pipes a year.

Port Types

Port, then, is wine which retains natural grape sugar because its fermentation has been stopped – before completion – by the addition of brandy. Every stage of its production is closely controlled. But this is only half of what we need to know. Port is rarely sold as 'Port': it will generally also carry a distinguishing style, such as Ruby Port, Tawny Port, or Vintage Port. Each of these terms will now be examined, and an explanation given as to what it means, and how each wine is made.

First, though, a word about the phrase 'wood port'. This term is used to signify those ports that complete their maturation cycle in wood, and are then bottled for immediate drinking. It is not a useful term: it has no clear opposite, and is therefore more likely to confuse than illuminate. Furthermore there are a number of types sold today that might not be thought wood ports, but that nevertheless achieve maturity in wood before being bottled ready to drink, such as many Late-Bottled·Vintage wines and all Vintage Character wines. Single Quinta wines are not wood ports – they are Vintage wines that mature in bottle – and yet in a number of cases they appear on the market only when considered

ready to drink by their shippers. Because of these and other ambiguities the phrase will be avoided.

Ruby Port

Ruby Port is a blended port made up of wines that are, on average, three years old. During that time it is aged in wood. It is then bottled early enough to retain the deep colour and lively fruit flavour of a young wine. After bottling, it is ready for immediate consumption, and will not improve any further, although it can safely be stored for up to a year. As the wines are filtered before bottling, they will not produce a deposit or need decanting.

This is the shipper's 'basic' port, and it should be as much a source of pride as the company's Vintage Ports are. If anything more so, because the preparation of basic blends, consistent from one year to the next regardless of weather conditions, is arguably more of a challenge than the preparation of Vintage Port, where nature has, by definition, done much of the work already.

Ruby and Tawny Ports are those for which much brand-building has had to be done by the

shippers over the last 30 or 40 years. Each brand will have a slightly different character, reflecting the shipper's own house style, and by trying a number of these you will generally find one that is to your taste. Labelling is simple, as only one word is legally necessary: Port (Porto in the USA and elsewhere), together with the shipper's name and address (if bottled in Portugal), bottle capacity, and the fact that the wine comes from Portugal. Few shippers are content to leave it at that, though, and in addition to the word 'Ruby' you will often see qualifying adjectives such as 'Fine Old' or 'Full Rich' on the label, too. These are permitted at present, but guarantee the consumer nothing, and should be ignored. It is the wine in the glass that matters.

Tawny Port

It should be said at the outset that there are two kinds of Tawny Port, and that the label on the bottle will give you little help in distinguishing one from the other. The most reliable way to do that is to look at the price tag.

If the wine seems expensive to you, that is to say if it costs perhaps double the price of a basic Ruby Port, then you may assume that it is a true Tawny. This is a port that has been wood-aged for anything between five and 50 years, so that it has lost its bright, plum-red colour and vigorous, peppery flavour, and has mellowed to a red/amber/orange – or 'tawny' – colour, and has acquired a smooth, light, slightly nutty flavour. Not all the wine will be 50 years old, nor will it all be five: it will be a blend of wines of different ages. The very best of these ports are classified in the group described below – Port with an indication of age – but there are also a number of excellent branded true Tawnies, such as Warre's 'Nimrod' or Delaforce's 'His Eminence's Choice', that rely on the shipper's name alone. It is worth mentioning here that fine Tawny is the port that the shippers themselves enjoy more often than any other: the wines represent the very best of their shipping and blending skills.

What of the other kind of Tawny Port, though? If the price of the bottle is similar to that of a basic Ruby Port, then it is, in all probability, a Port rosé: it will have been made by adding White Port to Ruby Port. The result tastes pleasant, and the pink-orange colour is attractive.

White Port is widely used in blending, to 'soften up' stern, tannic wines and add fragrance to aromatically dull wines, so there is nothing doubtful

about the practice itself. Furthermore, those shippers that use autovinification (see page 49) can now achieve light, easy 'Tawny' styles in young wines without the use of White Port.

The use of one word for both sorts of port, though – a young three year-old and an old wood-aged wine – is questionable, and it is a shame that the trade has not been able to come up with an alternative for the cheaper version. True Tawny Port must always be expensive: it needs long ageing, and holding large stocks of wine for decades is a costly business. Because customers are able to buy cheap 'Tawny Port', the word 'Tawny' no longer carries the aura that rightly belongs to this delicate and venerable wine.

Reading the label of a bottle of Tawny Port is, in principle, as simple as reading that on a bottle of Ruby. You need only look for two words: 'Tawny' and 'Port' (they can be in either order). It was mentioned above that price is the chief means of distinguishing the true Tawny from the rosé version, but the label will also give you hints, via the lavish language necessary as a consequence of the debasement of the word 'Tawny' itself. Warre's

MOST OF the Douro's finest quintas cling to the hillsides above and below Pinhão, and all are near the water – hence the old saying "If the wine is to be good, the grapes must hear the creak of the tiller".

'Nimrod', for example, is subtitled 'Very Finest Old Tawny – The Produce Of The Finest Vineyards Of The Douro Valley'. The term 'Very Finest Old Tawny' is not permitted on the labels of the younger (three year-old) kind of Tawny.

Port with an indication of age

Included under this rubric are the best of the Tawny Ports. You will never see these words on a label, but you will see one of four descriptions: '10 years old', '20 years old', '30 years old' or 'over 40 years old'. These are not Vintage Ports, so not every drop in a bottle of '30 years old' will be exactly that. Nor is it an average age; it is, rather, a blend tasted and approved as conforming to the characteristics of wines 30 years old. Labels must state that the wine has been matured in wood, and the date of bottling must be included on the front or back label.

The older the wine is, the more expensive you should expect it to be. Many port enthusiasts consider the '20 years old' to be the finest of all, while the '30 years old' and the 'over 40 years old' are of academic interest, not being sufficiently intense or astonishing to merit the price that must be asked for them. Any true port lover, though, should try all of these aromatic and silky wines at least once, and decide the merits of each for him or herself. They are ports like no others.

Dated or Colheita Ports

This type of port is rarely seen as yet in Britain, but is found more frequently in the rest of Europe and in the USA. Dated Ports are wines of a single year, aged in wood and bottled no less than seven winters later: a single year or vintage tawny, in other words. (The Portuguese word *colheita* means 'harvest' or 'crop', and by extension 'vintage'.) In addition to the vintage date, they must also carry the bottling date on the label or back label, together with statement of the fact that they have been matured in wood. The wines will throw no sediment and so will not need decanting, nor will they improve once bottled. Their quality can be and often is excellent, so long as it is remembered that they are from the Tawny rather than the Ruby or Vintage branch of the family. (The word *Novidade* was also formerly used to describe this style.)

Dated ports are often matured for great lengths of time – considerably longer than the seven year minimum – and some companies bottle only to order. Those who cherish the idea, or the act, of

drinking old wine should make some effort to seek them out – from some of the small non-British shippers specializing in this style. Burmester, for example, has 1922, 1937, 1944, 1955, 1963 and 1970 currently available, while Niepoort offers 1900, 1912, 1934, 1937, 1952, 1957, 1959, 1960, 1962, 1963, 1965, 1967, 1968, 1970, 1974 and many others.

White Port

White port is made in exactly the same way as red port, except that white grapes are used, and fermentation in the presence of the skins is for a limited period or not at all (as is the case with most white wines). It is a full-bodied, medium-sweet wine with a taste range that runs from grapiness to liquorice and almond flavours. The 'Dry' or even 'Very Dry' versions should be similar but less sweet. However shippers' brands vary enormously, and it is possible to find 'Very Dry' versions with noticeable residual sweetness, as well as plain 'White Port' that is comparatively dry to taste. Remember, too, that 'dry' is a relative term outside the port world as well as within it: no White Port will ever taste whistle dry, as does Fino or Manzanilla Sherry, for example. The port grapes and vinification methods are not suited to an austerely dry style. 'Light' versions of white port are also produced: these contain 17° of alcohol rather than 20°. Very sweet white dessert port is called Lacrima, Lacrima Cristi, Lacrima Sancta or Lacrima Divina.

Vintage Port

The best tunes are the simplest; the best ideas are the simplest. So with port: no style is simpler to make, or finer to drink (some 15 or 20 years later) than Vintage Port. It is a port of one harvest, the product of favoured vineyards in a splendid year. Its story goes something like this.

In the late autumn or winter after the vintage, the port shipper begins to sort out his wines in the *adega* (winery) or wine centre in the Alto Douro. He will already have some idea about how good a year it has been by the relative healthiness of the grapes, but tasting the new (and at this stage unpalatable) wine is all-important. The best wines will be marked as such and set aside, after transport (by lorry, no longer by boat) to Vila Nova de Gaia in the spring. Some initial blending, from among wines of that year only, may take place.

A full year passes. The shipper tastes constantly

THE DARKNESS and damp atmosphere of this cellar (above) provides perfect storage conditions for vintage and other bottle-aged ports. Hieroglyph-like shipper's marks and a mysterious mathematics combine to describe each wine's biography.

during this time, blends at discretion, and reflects. By no means every year is good enough to be 'declared a vintage': is this one? If the shipper feels a vintage is possible, samples of the intended blend must be submitted to the Port Wine Institute for approval, together with a statement of how much Vintage Port the shipper intends to make. Once approval is obtained, the shipper may then declare the vintage – if convinced that the wine still merits it. (There is no obligation to do so, if he feels it doesn't. The decision to declare a vintage is never lightly

reached, as the shipper knows that this is the wine on which his company's reputation stands or falls – in several decades' time.) Samples will go to major customers, and the wine will be bottled during the summer, autumn or following spring, and shipped some months after that.

The customer then takes over. The wine should be kept in good cellar conditions (see Part Three) for at least ten years, and 15 or 20 are counselled for a top vintage. The port can then be opened, decanted and savoured, so completing the circle.

A Vintage Port wine label is straightforward: beneath the shipper's name the vintage will be given, together with the word 'Vintage' or the words 'Vintage Port'. The *selo de garantia* slip will be visible beneath the capsule. This, in effect, is all you need to look for, though there may be further information included on the label, such as the year in which the port was bottled (two or three years after the vintage).

Late-Bottled Vintage Port

Late-Bottled Vintage (or LBV, as it is often known) is also port of a single year. The rules require the year to be 'of good quality'; in practice, this generally means the next-best years to those declared as vintages, though a recent trend suggests that LBVs may in future appear as 'second-label' ports from a declared vintage year. The wines are kept for nearly four years in wood, before being bottled sometime between this and their sixth birthday: the 'late bottling' referred to in their name.

Further generalization about these wines is difficult, however, because much depends on the practices of the shipper. Some shippers will bottle as early as possible without filtration, and may even use wines originally registered with the IVP as Vintage Port, but not subsequently declared. In this case, the wines will throw a sediment, and continue to improve for some six to eight years in bottle. They will always be lighter in colour than Vintage Port, but will exhibit much of its complexity – and will be excellent value for money. Driven corks, rather than cork stopper tops, are an indicator of this sort of LBV. Look out, too, for a bottling date during the fourth year, rather than the fifth or sixth year, after the vintage. Warre and Smith Woodhouse, who make a speciality of this sort of LBV, refer to the wines as 'traditional Late-Bottled Vintage' (though they cannot do this on the labels as the qualification is not legally recognized).

Most shippers, though, wait as long as possible before bottling, and filter immediately before doing so. Wines of this sort will not throw a deposit or need decanting, and will not improve much with age. As one disenchanted shipper put it, "A wine that's spent six years in cask is already a tawny." Others regard them as dated 'Vintage Character' wines. They are, though, for these very reasons, a popular choice with restaurateurs. Diners may be misled into thinking they are true Vintage Ports by inadequately explicit – or deliberately inexplicit – wine lists.

Late-Bottled Vintage, then, can be seen as 'convenience port': a vintage date, but no waiting or decanting. Those acquainted with the glories of true Vintage Port throw up their hands in horror at this modern aberration, and in some ways rightly so. But the practice of late bottling is neither modern or aberrant: all the great pre-phylloxera vintages were, by the letter of today's laws, late-bottled, after four or so years in wood. The wines, it is said, were bigger then, and needed the extra two years' wood softening before going into glass.

The regulations governing the labelling of LBVs are detailed on several points. The words 'Late-Bottled Vintage' or 'L.B.V.' must appear on one line only, with each word or letter printed in the same type and colour, and the vintage date must always be followed by the bottling date (optional in the case of Vintage Port). The object of this, it is claimed, is to avoid any possible confusion with Vintage Port, though of course the wines sell on just such a confusion. This is causing serious concern to many people in the port trade, and there is a possibility that in the future the style may simply become 'Late Bottled' or 'L.B.', with no mention of 'Vintage' other than the date of harvest itself.

Crusting or Crusted Port

Here is another port type that, like LBV, was created to appeal to the Vintage Port enthusiast of modest means. This enthusiast, though, has patience, a cellar or storage area, some relish of the decanting ritual, and does not require a vintage date on the label. The wines may be those of a single year, but in practice they tend to be a blend of wines from different years, bottled young (between three to four years after the harvest) without filtration. They continue to improve in bottle for another five years or so, throwing a light 'crust' (deposit or sediment) as they do so – hence the name, the patience, and the relish for decanting.

shortcomings, and as the IVP does not yet officially recognize this style, there will be no *selo de garantia* to reassure the drinker either. (For the same reason, the wines cannot be bottled in Portugal, but are in general bottled in Britain.) All you will see in addition to the key words 'Crusting' or 'Crusted Port' will be the shipper's name and address and the bottling date.

This type of port was in the doldrums during the 1970s, and at one point it looked as if the more 'convenient' LBVs and Vintage Character wines would jostle it into extinction. Happily this has not happened, and these wines are once again enjoying a discreet popularity. Given adequate time to knit, they should not disappoint.

Even here, sadly, a note of caution is required. Some Crusting Ports are now being cold-filtered before bottling, and will therefore be little better than many LBVs or Vintage Character wines, neither developing in bottle nor throwing a proper crust. There is no hard-and-fast rule for spotting these: if in doubt, consult the Directory of Port Shippers on pages 56–71, in which reliable producers of Crusting Port are noted. It is to be hoped that, when recognition by the IVP is achieved, the rules will outlaw cold-filtering for this style.

In today's market, Crusting Ports and Single Quinta Ports (see below) offer the two top value alternatives to Vintage Port. Crusting Ports are the less fashionable of the two, and are therefore likely to be best value of all. Because they need decanting, restaurants are reluctant to stock them (if they must decant, they would prefer to decant the more profitable Vintage Ports). More importantly, though, is the challenge Crusting Ports represent to the shipper. Unlike Single Quinta Ports, Crusting Ports require the shipper's best blending skills: he must find a number of high-quality young ports, and assemble them into a blend that will knit together over three or more years in bottle to form a port of character and panache. These wines will then stand or fall on the shipper's name. No vintage or vineyard details are given on the label to account for possible

Single Quinta Port

'Quinta' (pronounced 'kinta') is the Portuguese word for farm, estate, property – and by extension, vineyard. Single Quinta Ports are therefore single vineyard ports. But – and this is important to remember – they are also Vintage Ports, and will always carry a vintage date. Samples have to be submitted to the IVP as for Vintage Port, and the wines are also bottled when two or three years old, as for Vintage Port. They will throw a crust in the bottle, and will need decanting. Indeed some shippers' Vintage Ports are always Single Quinta Ports: Quinta do Noval Vintage and Offley Forrester's

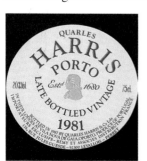

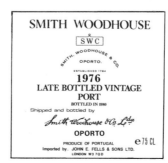

*B*UILDINGS JOSTLE for space, behind Vila Nova de Gaia's once-busy waterfront (above).

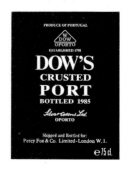

Boa Vista Vintage are examples. In the future, small growers may also export their own Vintage Port, which will be *de facto* Single Quinta port: two examples already exported are Miguel Champalimaud's Quinta do Côtto and Antonio Vinagre's Quinta da Romaneira.

In most cases, though, there are two differences between a shipper's Single Quinta and his Vintage Ports. The first, and most important, is that the Single Quinta Port will only be produced in second-rank years, the sort of years from which a shipper has traditionally considered producing an LBV. In fine years, the wines of the Quinta in question (the best that a shipper may own or have access to) will form the core of the shipper's Vintage Port. So Single Quinta Ports should not be expected to rival Vintage Ports: they are simpler wines, although characterful and fascinating – often the key to a shipper's 'house style'.

The second difference is that they are often only released when the shipper considers them ready to drink, some nine or ten years after the harvest. This makes them a particularly good buy for those who find it difficult to keep unopened bottles at home in their unopened state, or for those with no cellar facilities.

Labels are similar to the shipper's Vintage Port label, except that the Quinta name will be clearly visible above the vintage date. Details of shippers' major Quinta holdings are to be found in Part Two of the book.

Ports of this sort can be excellent value for money. They are consequently attracting great interest at the moment, and it seems likely that more of these wines will appear on the market in the future, especially now that port can be exported direct from the Douro, rather than – as before 1986 – having to pass through the entrepôt of Vila Nova de Gaia. The way is open for small quinta owners to ship their own vintage wine direct to export markets.

In every area of wine production and appreciation today, there is a trend away from the blended product and towards the individualized wine: the wine of character, reflecting particular soils, a particular microclimate, a particular year. Paradoxically, this success may cause the big shippers problems, as in the past the wines of their top quintas, in less-than-perfect years, have been used for fine Tawnies and Crusted Ports, and are now also needed for LBVs and Vintage Character wines. If Single Quinta ports continue to grow in popularity at their present rate, there may not be enough to go around, and the quality of these other wines will begin to fall. This is one of the reasons that new plantings are seen every year in the best areas of the Alto Douro.

There is, though, another reason. In the past, Single Quinta wines did not have to come exclusively from the quinta concerned: legally, they were only subject to the same geographical constraints as Vintage Port. The use of the word 'Quinta' was a matter for the shipper's integrity – which is why Graham's Malvedos was only 'Malvedos' and not 'Quinta dos Malvedos'. In the future, this is to change: Single Quinta wine will have to be single vineyard (or, more accurately, single property) wine. The shippers are busy planting to full capacity to prepare for this, so there will be a lot of young vines in the top quintas over the next two decades. Quality should not be affected . . . but that again will be a matter for the shipper's integrity.

Garrafeira *Port*

This port is almost exclusively consumed in Portugal, and is seen abroad infrequently. Portuguese table wine enthusiasts will be familiar with the word *garrafeira*: it connotes something like 'merchant's pride' – specially selected wines from several regions but of one vintage, blended together and given long bottle ageing before being sold (10- or 15-year-old *garrafeira* table wines are common in Portugal). As the word carries such prestige with the Portuguese purchaser, it obviously makes commercial sense to extend its use to port. Ports so styled are wines of a single vintage (though not necessarily an outstanding year) that have received long cask and bottle ageing – or, in the case of Niepoort (see page 64), ageing in glass demijohns – before being decanted off their sediment, rebottled and sold. (This makes them, in terms of port wine law, a subdivision of Dated or *Colheita* Ports.) The best *Garrafeiras* are

elegant, lacy ports of considerable age (Niepoort is currently selling 1931, 1938, 1940, 1948, 1950 and 1952). Port aficionados should not miss tasting them.

Vintage Character, Style or Reserve

This is, in most cases, premium Ruby Port. A bottle of Vintage Character Port contains a blend of wines from different vintages that have been aged in wood for an average of five years, filtered and bottled. It may contain wines up to six or seven years old, and generally contains wines from the better parts of the Alto Douro. The final blend is unlikely to improve in bottle, and the wine is meant for immediate consumption, without decanting.

These are in the main enjoyable, well-made ports, but like LBV rarely justify the use of the word 'Vintage' on the label, or the comparison this invites. The legal requirement that sanctions the misleading labelling of these ports is the fact that no date can ever appear with descriptions of the 'Vintage Character' sort. But, as with LBV, the damage is already done, the association already made, in print, on the label. It requires deduction to differentiate between the word 'Vintage' and the absence of a date, and most wine purchasers do not possess the necessary scepticism to make such a deduction. They are being misled.

They do not mind, of course, because they do not feel cheated: the wines are fair value for money, and the label impresses their friends. It is the good name of Vintage Port that suffers, and it is strange to see the port trade as a whole damage the image of its finest product in this way.

So much for the name. What of the wine in the bottles? Vintage Character Port has an older pedigree than modern LBV, having been produced and marketed as long ago as the 1920s; in the 1980s, though, the style has become uneven in quality, thanks largely to the cut-throat trading of supermarket 'own-brand' Vintage Character Ports. The quality of some of these – priced within a whisker of ordinary Ruby – has disturbed those shippers producing top-quality Vintage Character Ports, and serious questions are being asked about the future of the style in Oporto. Several shippers have chosen not to compete at all, instead building a brand that will stand on its own, they hope, in the public's estimation – and provide a better glass of port at a similar price.

To summarize, then: there are some very poor Vintage Character Ports, cheaply priced; there are some good Vintage Character Ports, fairly priced; and there are some good alternatives. See the Directory of Port Shippers (pages 56–71) for producers of wines in the last two categories.

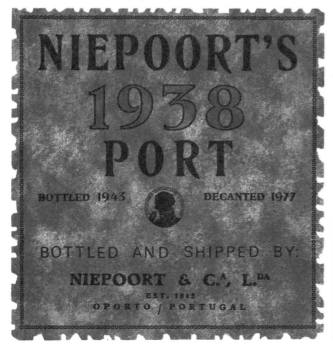

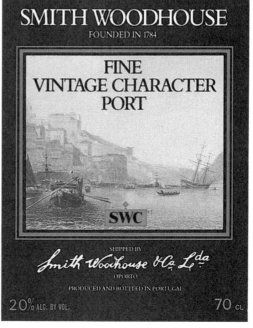

PART TWO

Port Production

In Part One of the book, port was defined in the abstract. The various types of port were examined, thus showing port theory put into practice. What hasn't been described yet is the in-between stage: exactly how this happens. How is it that sap rising in vine stumps in a remote part of Portugal every summer is turned into an inky purple wine requiring up to 20 years' confinement in a glass cell before it is ready to drink? This is the general question discussed in this Part of the book.

> *"He offered me port, I remember, as the proper milk of youth . . ."*
> **Robert Louis Stevenson**
> *(Talk and Talkers)*

Two aspects of the history of port have already been narrated: the development of port drinking from the times of the crusaders to our own day, and the development of port legislation, stemming from Pombal's 18th-century reforms. The one important historical aspect that has not been considered in detail yet is the development of the wine itself: how port as we now know it evolved from the 'red Portugal' of crusading times.

The century that separates the appointment of an English consul in Viana do Castelo (north of Oporto) in 1578, and the first recorded shipment of 'Vinho do Porto' from Oporto in 1678 would have seen the birth of the wine now known as port. Viana is in the Minho, of course, and at the time this first consul got his posting all the wines exported would have been the light 'red Portugal' discussed above and in the Introduction. These wines did not travel well, as we know, and were not popular in England; French claret and red Florence were preferred. The latter, in particular, was a wine of deep colour and high strength, and suited those living in cold, damp England perfectly.

Fate, though, seems to have been on port's side. Red Florence suffered from severe quality-control problems: the Italians used chestnut wood for their casks, and these were so porous that much wine was lost and spoilt in transit. They tried importing it in flasks, but as the flasks were sealed with nothing more substantial than a small ladleful of olive oil, the results were not much better. "Do you know," wrote Jonathan Swift to Stella (Esther Johnson), "that my whole chest of Florence is turned sour, at least the first two flasks were, and hardly drinkable? How plaguy unfortunate am I!"

Claret, meanwhile, was dealt a series of political blows, as a trade war broke out in Louis XIV's time that resulted in prohibitive duties being imposed on all French wines. Trade wars became real wars, and claret was soon unpatriotic as well as unobtainable. Swift took to port:

Be sometimes to your country true,
Have once the public good in view:
Bravely despise Champagne at Court
And choose to dine at home with Port.

The oldest alliance

English and later British patriotism had, in fact, always sanctioned port drinking, not only on account of the number of Britons working in the wine trade in Portugal. A Treaty of Perpetual Friendship was signed as early as 1386, ratifying an earlier (lost) treaty of 1151. This 'Perpetual Friendship' was invoked and confirmed in 1943, to general astonishment, when Portugal allowed the British to use the Azores as a naval and air base, despite her own neutrality in World War II. During the period that concerns us here, it was Portugal that needed British help: Philip II of Spain had subjugated the country, and the period the Portuguese call 'The Captivity' had begun. Apart from defeating Philip's Armada in 1588, England could offer the Portuguese no more than sentimental friendship at this time, for Portugal was part of Spain and Spain was the enemy. There were still English, Scottish and Irish wine merchants in Portugal. Little is known for sure about their activities, but much of the Minho was ravaged during 'The Captivity', and it is believed that this was the point at which the Douro was first explored and considered by the British for wine-growing. (Vines have grown in the Douro since the Bronze Age and earlier, and wines have been made there from Roman times onwards.)

THE CATHEDRAL at the town of Lamego – the possible birthplace of port as we know it today.

Portugal was proclaimed a sovereign state again in 1640. The new king, João IV, faced many problems at home and abroad: the Spanish had by no means relinquished their pan-Iberian aspirations, and much of the Portuguese Empire in the Far East had been lost. He needed a strong ally and so, despite kingly misgivings about befriending a regicide, he turned to Oliver Cromwell.

The treaty of 1654, signed with Cromwell, placed English merchants in Portugal in an extremely favourable position. They enjoyed numerous trading privileges there, while the home country provided a large and thirsty market on which they had a near monopoly for all the wine they could export. There was money to be made, and plenty of it. The only difficulty was in ensuring that adequate supplies of good wine reached the taverns of Fleet Street and Ludgate Hill in palatable form.

What was wanted was strong, dark wine. The Douro region could produce this; the Minho could not. The Douro, therefore, became the focus of the British wine trade in Portugal from this point onwards . . . and so to that first recorded shipment out of Oporto in 1678.

That year 408 pipes made the sea journey northwards. This was quite a lot of wine, and therefore almost certainly not the first ever out of Oporto. Included amongst it may have been a few rather special pipes, bound for the city of Liverpool.

The Abbot's secret

A nameless Liverpool wine merchant had sent his two sons to Viana to learn the wine trade. In the summer of that year, 1678, they journeyed to the Douro, spending the night at a monastery at Lamego, a little to the south of Régua. There the Abbot served them some of his own wine from Pinhão, a town 25 kilometres upriver, and in the heart of today's port wine country. The brothers liked this wine so much that they bought as much as they could.

What did it taste like? Unfortunately the story varies on this important point. Some hold that it was merely a table wine, made with characteristic monastic excellence. Others assert that it had a rich, smooth, slightly sweet flavour: made by the Abbot himself, who told his guests that he had added locally produced brandy to the wine during its fermentation. If so, then this Portuguese Dom Pérignon is the father of port, and 1678 is a date no port lover should forget.

The brothers must have forgotten what the Abbot told them, though, as fortification was practised only after fermentation for some decades to come. Perhaps the rigours of their journey wiped this vital detail from their minds. Thomas Woodmass, another young merchant travelling up the Douro 25 years later, describes the advisability in this area of "sleeping on ye tables for reason of ye vermin." His earlier journey down from Viana had not been without incident:

> We bestrode mules with awkward straw stuf'd saddles, and with us came 2 murderous looking men to beat our mules .... using much noise and many othes to keep ye half-starv'd mules agoing, but when we were as half way between Viana and Fon my mule did roll with me, and shortly it was discover'd she was dead, so ye rest on foot. At Fon I procured a horse from ye Priest which did kick for reason of ye flies, but he was not ill fed. It was our intention to stay over ye night at Villadecon but it was not so to be, for 6 arm'd men did stop us in ye King's name, and examined our pockets, taking all we had; all but our long coats and hats, and then tied each one to a tree with his arms behind in which sorry plite we were fain to spend ye night until ye next morning, when our 3 rascalls, coming as if by chance, cutt ye cords and we were again free.

A diabolical practice

Evidence supporting the possibility that the Abbot of Lamego invented port comes, ironically, from a shippers' complaint of 1754.

> The grower at the time of the Vintage, is in the habit of checking the fermentation of the wines too soon, by putting brandy into them while still fermenting; a practice which must be considered DIABOLICAL, for after this the wines will not remain quiet, but are continually tending to ferment and to become ropy and acid.

The growers obviously had the right idea, and this idea must have come from somewhere: why not Lamego? The unfortunate refermentation, though, suggests that insufficient brandy was used, or brandy of insufficient strength – or indeed some other problem altogether, perhaps connected with cellar hygiene. The shippers at this point, in any case, were sure that what they wanted was sturdy red table wine, and it was sturdy red table wine, fortified after fermentation, that they shipped back to London. Coarse, harsh, heavy stuff:

> Mark how it smells. Methinks, a real pain
> Is by its odour thrown upon my brain.

So wrote Richard Ames of a pint of his local tavern's "best Red Port". It still had little more than patriotism in its favour.

Enter Pombal. As we know from the section on port legislation in Part One, Pombal's monopoly company improved the quality of port greatly, and some steps towards standardization of port production must have been taken then. Of equal impor-

*T*HE DUKE of Wellington had happy memories of Oporto: as Sir Arthur Wellesley he routed Napoleon's Marshal Soult there in May 1809, using a surprise attack from Vila Nova de Gaia.

tance was the evolution, between 1770 and 1793, of the modern glass bottle. Until this period, glass bottles had been squat and dumpy in shape, like bulbous ship's decanters. More jug than bottle, they were designed to transport wine from the cask in which it was shipped to the table at which it was drunk – and not to slop or topple over if the company got too boisterous. They could not, of course, be stored on their sides. The significance of this fact is hard to underestimate: it meant that true vintage wines did not exist. The only containers available for ageing wines were casks. Wines age rapidly in cask because they are exposed to air, and they have to be topped up regularly with wines from subsequent vintages, thus becoming blended wines. Only when the great-great-grandfather of the long, narrow-shouldered modern bottle appeared in 1770 did vintage port, or vintage anything, become possible. The wine could now be locked in its glass cell with cork, stored on its side, and the liquid would keep the cork moist, ensuring a perfect seal (dry cork shrinks). Port historians have considered

*D*ona antónia *Adelaide
Ferreira (1811–1896)
took over the running of her
late husband's company in
1844, and quickly transformed
it from a small concern to one
of the biggest and most
important of all port shippers.
Eighteen years later she
escaped unscathed from the
river accident that claimed*

*Baron Forrester's life –
thanks to her crinoline.*

centre for all British merchants (or 'factors' – those trading on behalf of others; hence 'Factory' – a trading station maintained by factors in a foreign country). The distinguished granite building, wholly British in the severity and solidity of its architecture, was later taken over exclusively by the wine shippers, who remain in occupation to this day.

An unusual shipper

In 1831, in the middle of the Portuguese 'War of the Two Brothers', a 22 year-old Englishman from Hull disembarked at Oporto. His name was Joseph James Forrester, and he had come to Portugal to join his uncle's port shipping firm of Offley Forrester and Company.

The first thing young Mr Forrester did after reaching Portugal marked him out as an unusual shipper: he learnt Portuguese. All the subsequent actions and achievements of this prodigiously talented man were stamped with the same singularity: he made friends with the Portuguese, high and low; he produced hand-drawn maps of the region that any professional cartographer of the time would have envied; he produced watercolours and oil paintings of the region and of Oporto; he wrote and illustrated monographs on every aspect of port production and viticulture in general (an essay on pests and diseases of the vine was adopted by the Royal Society); he invented an improved method of extracting olive oil from olives; he made a collection of earthenware figures representing all the regional costumes of the country; and he prepared a pamphlet, in 1844, called 'A Word or Two on Port Wine'.

The contents of this pamphlet were as explosive as its title was unassuming. Forrester accused his colleagues in the port trade of numerous malpractices, among them adulteration of the wines with *baga* (the infamous elderberry juice), *geropiga* (today a very sweet port used for blending purposes, but at that time a ferocious mixture of dried elderberries, brown sugar, treacle, grape juice and brandy) and with sugar. The pamphlet contained other serious allegations concerning corruption within Pombal's Companhia, still in existence at this time, and there can be little doubt but that most of them were true. The shipping establishment countered with the pusillanimous reply heard time and time again from merchants of every sort accused of fraud or malpractice: "It's what the customer wants". The dust took some time to settle.

the first great port vintage to be 1775, and in this as in other respects port led the way for the world's other fine wines.

It seems likely that, at this stage, port fermentation was being stopped by the addition of brandy – but not in every case, and not without controversy, as we will discover in a moment. Trade was excellent, which indicates that the wine was at last popular on its own merits with the drinking public, and the future looked bright; bright and secure enough for the building of the Factory House in Oporto, between 1786 and 1790. This acted as a

THIS ENGRAVING of Oporto (above) in 1835 is taken from a drawing by Baron Forrester, and was published by Forrester himself. It makes his superb draughtsmanship plain, and evinces his interest in regional costume.

THE CHANGING shape of the port bottle (below) – from the squat, dumpy bottle of the 1700s to the long, narrow-shouldered bottle of today.

Most significant of all, though, was Forrester's assertion that port should be a 'natural' wine, a wine whose fermentation had not been stopped with brandy. Forrester may have been misguided on this point, but we know from his criticism that the practice of arresting fermentation with brandy was common by 1844. It can not have been uniformly successful, or Forrester would have had few grounds for criticism, but it must have been common. Port was, more or less, port.

The port trade and the Portuguese later forgave Forrester the honesty of his opinions, and he was made a Baron by the King of Portugal for his services to wine.

The Baron's death, at the age of 53, was as dramatic as his life had been. In 1862, returning down the Douro after lunching at the Quinta de Vargellas with Baroness Fladgate (of Taylor, Fladgate and Yeatman) and Dona Antónia Adelaide Ferreira (of Ferreira), the boat hit a rock in the rapids of the Cachão da Valeira and foundered. The ladies' crinolines kept them afloat in the turbulent waters, and they were washed onto the river bank little the worse for the experience. Forrester, though, was hit by a mast, and was further hampered by the leather money belt he was wearing, containing wages (in the form of gold sovereigns) for his farmers. The official account of the incident has it that his body was never found. His son William, though, was told that his father's corpse had been washed up early one morning at Pinhão, the money belt removed, and the body sunk again.

Was his death deliberate? Forrester had remarked as they entered the gorge that the tiller was lashed the wrong way, but negligence seems more likely than homicide. There are surely easier ways of parting a man from his money belt.

The brandy question

Port was now port, and the major waymarks in its evolution had been located and passed. It was now fortified during fermentation, and aged in both wood and bottle. Many difficulties still lay ahead for its producers: wars and sieges, floods, corruption, market changes, and worst of all the phylloxera scourge, examined in the next section. It seems appropriate, though, brandy having finally won its place in port, to examine the 'brandy question' by way of conclusion to this section.

Brandy question? 'Brandy controversy' would be a more appropriate phrase. It was Forrester himself who first publicly queried brandy's presence in port, not long after it had become accepted and customary. Connoisseurs and purists continue to question it to this day.

The Victorian wine writer Cyrus Redding, in his *History of Modern Wines*, castigated the addition of brandy to what he felt was an already over-adulterated wine. The early 20th-century connoisseur and merchant, Charles Walter Berry, refused, as others before and since, to admit that port was a wine at all. At the conclusion of a Burgundy dinner attended by the wine writer H. Walter Allen, Berry served the fine, scarce vintage port of 1815, the 'Waterloo'. While his guests enjoyed it, Berry himself finished a magnum of Romanée–Conti 1868, begun earlier in the evening. (He did not carry purism so far as to neglect to elicit his guests' superlatives on the port.)

In 1985, the wine writer Nicholas Faith put a new complexion on the old controversy, singling out vintage port as the most villainous of the family.

Faith's contention is that the brandy in vintage port, after only two years in wood, is still 'raw' (brandy, unlike wine, does not age or develop in any way in glass). The two components, he asserts, never properly marry, and the fine wine is rendered disagreeable by the crude spirit, which is why "Vintage port must, logically, be a coarse and vile drink, unworthy of the attention of connoisseurs." Tawny port he admires ("an altogether admirable drink"), as its longer wood ageing has mellowed the fiery spirit, allowing the wine's components to marry productively.

A line of criticism unexplored by Faith concerns the quality of the spirit, rather than its age or maturity. The wine in a bottle of vintage port is the finest the Douro has to offer, while the brandy is simply a Portuguese grape spirit distinguished only by its neutrality. By what alchemy can this base material be transformed into something gloriously drinkable? Or is it all a confidence trick? as Faith suggests. "In Oporto the local shippers naturally prefer tawny port although they are not going to deter anyone from paying exorbitant sums for the vintage rubbish."

If it is a confidence trick, it is one of the world's most successful examples ever. Can so many people have been duped for so long?

The answer is 'no': if vintage port was truly 'coarse and vile' then the shippers would not be able to sell it. Customers might purchase one bottle, but they would be unlikely to repeat the experience. There are, though, people who do not like port, or vintage port, just as there are people who do not like fish or strawberries. If they are wine enthusiasts, then brandy is the scapegoat on which they vent their frustration. The fineness of the wine is evident, so it must be the brandy that is at fault.

In fact the key to brandy's role in port lies precisely in its neutrality. Shippers select brandy that is as clean and characterless as possible. Brandy can then, to use a fanciful analogy, act as the canvas on which port's picture-in-flavour is painted. Its role is an enabling one: no canvas, no picture; no brandy, no port. Having made the painting possible, it should then be present as a texture or surface only; all the colour and excitement is provided by the paint, the fruit, the wine. This is a response to those who question brandy's role in port.

To the more technical question about the mellowing of brandy in vintage port, the practical response is that it is partly mystery and partly a matter of taste. A mysterious marriage of flavours

does take place in mature vintage port; but it may not be to your taste. The neutrality of the spirit should not be overlooked: it is fine, characterful spirits full of 'congenerics' (flavourful impurities) like Cognac, Armagnac and whisky that demand wood ageing; neutral spirits like vodka or gin do not. Nor should it be forgotten that the neutral grape brandy is diluted in powerfully flavoured, partly-fermented port wine. The spirit matures in wine rather than in glass. As postscript, one should add that port shippers do not in fact prefer tawny port to vintage: "Tawny certainly for everyday drinking, but vintage whenever we wish to 'push the boat out' in even a modest manner," responded shipper Michael Symington to Faith's remarks.

WHITE QUINTA buildings (above) break the impressive monotony of these Upper Douro vineyards near Pinhão.

THE BEST-KNOWN portrait of Joseph James – later Baron – Forrester shows him as a young man, plainly dressed and physically unprepossessing (right). The intelligence of his eyes and the determined set of his chin, though, suggest what biography confirms: talent, and the drive necessary for realizing talent.

From vineyard to lodge

It is the first of November. A wine farmer stands on one of the lower terraces of his quinta in the Alto Douro. River and railway lie below him; behind and around him lines of terraces stretch up to form a high horizon. The heat of the summer has passed. There is a fretful wind blowing, and heavy grey clouds scud across the sky, suggesting that rain is on the way. Many of the leaves have been chased from the vines by the wind, and from time to time a gust draws a leafy column into the air before dropping it nonchalantly onto the terrace below.

This is the turning point of the vineyard year. The harvest is over. The new wines will be resting in their *toneis* (large wooden casks) after the excitements of fermentation and fortification. In the vineyard, everything begins all over again.

Rain is on the way – or so the farmer hopes, and as much of it as possible, for the vines are parched at this point. Indeed the first job that has to be

BUILDING NEW terraces on mountainsides is an awesome task. Machinery helps today; most of the Douro's terraces were built by pickaxe, muscle and sweat.

completed is the digging of trenches around the vines to catch as much water during the winter as possible: the *escava d'agua*. The wines enjoy limited fertilization (with small quantities of nitrogen, phosphorus and potassium) at this point. Delicate judgement is required: too much will result in overproduction and a consequent fall in quality, while too little will mean lower quality too, as the vine struggles without resources to produce the best fruit the weather permits.

Between November and January the *podadores*, or pruners, arrive at the quinta. They are skilled workers: a badly pruned vine could have disastrous effects on the following year's harvest, as well as on the vine's long-term productivity. The pruning is ruthless: only two grape-bearing canes are left to provide the following year's fruit. The *podadores*, working through the winter, require copious quantities of *bagaceira* (local marc, distilled from port pomace: the skins and pips that remain

after wine-making) to keep out the cold.

In the bleak months of December and January, little else besides pruning can be done in the vineyards. The wines themselves are still resting, so cleaning and maintenance, attention to other crops, or even some well-deserved holiday will occupy the farmer at this time.

In February and March the workers return to the vineyards. This is the period for the building of new terraces, for the planting of American rootstocks and for grafting year-old plantings.

Why, you may wonder, are there American rootstocks in a Douro vineyard? The answer is that without them, there would simply be no vineyards in the Douro, or across most of Europe. Wine as we know it would not exist. American rootstocks have made 20th-century viticulture possible.

The phylloxera disaster

In 1863, a cluster of tiny insects was discovered on a vine in a wealthy London businessman's greenhouse in Hammersmith. They were sent to Professor Westwood at Oxford, who examined them with great interest. Barely visible without magnification, they seemed little more than an entomological curiosity at first. They proved to be a parasite of unparalleled viciousness. Within 20 years it was a near-certainty that production of quality wine, in quantity, would soon finish for all time. The same insect, now named *phylloxera vastatrix*, had systematically destroyed every vineyard in Europe, and it would soon travel the world. In its wake it left leaves disfigured by galls, acid and sugarless grapes and – eventually – dead vines with black, rotting roots. It left wine growers penniless, vineyards deserted. The growers made for the cities, or emigrated, to find a living; many of their vineyards remain deserted to this day.

Phylloxera first appeared in the Douro – at Gouvinhas – in 1868. It took hold more slowly there than elsewhere. But the effect was soon felt: at the Quinta do Oliveirinho, production of 38 pipes in 1875 was cut to only eight three years later; and none at all the year after that. The end of the port trade was being openly discussed by 1881.

The pest had come from Eastern America, and it was from there that the solution to this seemingly insoluble problem came. All European native wine vine varieties – and all fine wine varieties the world over – belong to the *vitis vinifera* family. Vitis vinifera is defenceless against phylloxera. But there are other vine families native to the same habitat as

*T*HE TINY *insect (below),*
phylloxera vastatrix,
*responsible for the destruction
of many European vineyards.
About 0.3 of a millimetre in
length, it proved to be a
diminutive but vicious pest.*

*T*HE RIVER *Tua joins the
Douro beneath the
railway bridge, two stations
east of Pinhão (above). The
Douro is often thought to be a
monocultural region, but the
other crops growing on the
fertile river bank show that
this is not strictly true.*

*C*OCKBURN HAS *developed
a large area of flat,
though schistous, land
adjacent to the River Vilariça
in the eastern high Douro
(left). These newly planted
vines will be among the first
in the Douro to be tended –
perhaps even picked – by
mechanical means.*

the louse that have, over the centuries, become resistant to it. One such is the American vine *vitis rupestris*. By using vinifera vines grafted onto rupestris roots, the insect can be defeated. Not permanently: it is still present in most wine-growing areas, and reappears wherever American rootstocks are not used. (With one exception: vines grown in sand dunes, as in Portugal's Colares area, are safe, for phylloxera cannot prosper in sand.)

It is for this reason that, every February and March, new American vines are planted in the Douro vineyards to replace old vines that have reached the end of their useful life, or to provide new vineyards on new terraces. They spend a year establishing themselves in the soil, and are then cut right back to the root at a point about 20 cm (8 in) beneath soil level; the vinifera variety is grafted onto this, bound with raffia, and the soil replaced. Grafting is another highly skilled task, requiring the services of an *enxertador*, or specialist vine-grafter.

The most spectacular task of the whole year is the building of new terraces. To understand why, it is necessary to know a little about the soil of the Alto Douro.

Platforms of schist

'Soil' is a misnomer, except in the most technical sense. Douro vines grow among lumps of broken rock. The rock is a dull grey-brown in colour, sometimes gravelly, sometimes slab-like: hard terrain to walk over, harder terrain still to work. It is schist: a mineral-rich, fissile stone of igneous origin. It is another secret of port production, for the best port is always made from grapes grown on schist. This is partly due to the favourable mineral composition of this slowly decomposing stone, and partly due to its excellent water-retaining properties. The winter rains leach into the schist as into some enormous slaty sponge, and the deep-rooted vines can draw on these reserves during the rainless summer months.

The steep hillsides, before terracing, are covered with huge outcrops and platforms of schist. That is why, ever since Alfred Nobel's invention of 1867, this remote and normally quiet region has often sounded like a rebel zone of Portugal under siege, with explosion succeeding explosion the length of a calm February afternoon. This has been the only way to break up the rock to a degree workable enough to permit terrace construction, and then subsequently to prepare the 'soil' itself.

V ERTICAL DRY stone walls to support terraces, as in this photograph taken in the late 19th century (above), have not been constructed since 1970. Terraces are no longer walled: the rock is left bare and sloping, and vegetation binds the terrace.

A TINY vine is planted in rock (right). Its mysterious survival and later fruition remain matters of wonder.

Even after the dynamite had done its work, the manpower needed to complete a hillside of terraces was colossal. Nowadays huge bulldozers assist in this task.

There are two types of new terrace under construction in the Alto Douro: inclined and horizontal terraces. The former are the wider of the two and, as their name suggests, slope gently. They are cheaper to construct than horizontal terraces as fewer are needed on a hillside, and more rows of vines can be planted on each. On the horizontal terraces only two to four rows of vines can be planted; nevertheless they are the favoured type, as mechanization (and particularly the use of the *enjambeur* tractor, which straddles vines) is possible on them. Mechanization of the vineyards is becoming a key factor in the Alto Douro: despite the

unpromising terrain, this will be the only way to keep prices at a reasonable level in the future. Every stage of port production has traditionally been labour-intensive, but labour is no longer as cheap or plentiful as it once was, and it will be less so in the future. The old terraces, sometimes only one row of vines wide and each connected to the next by rows of steps, are impossible to work mechanically, and will be seen less and less frequently as the years go by.

April and May are always critical months in the Douro vineyard. This is the period during which the buds break and the vines flower. As the flowers fade, tiny bunches of grapes are formed. If pollination has been successful, then these pip-sized grapes will begin their long swelling and ripening process. If, however, there is a patch of bad weather during this time – late frosts, heavy rains, strong winds – then

THE SUPERB Egyptian profile of this 16-terrace hillside is lent drama by sun and shadow (above). Aspect is an important feature of Douro vineyards, but not overridingly so, thanks to the region's generous climate.

VINE-SPRAYING (right), as here at Taylor's Quinta de Vargellas, is an essential spring and summer task if the crop of grapes is to be healthy.

the process can fail altogether. Great vintages may be made in September and October, but the difference between a large and a small vintage can often be traced back to April and May.

The painter's visit

June, July, August, September: the vintage approaches. June 24th, St John's Day, is a special date in the Douro calendar: it is around then that *o pintor* (the painter) is said by the local people to arrive in the vineyards, leaving the first delicate brushstrokes of colour on the grapes. The vineyard workers tramp prosaically after him, spraying with a range of fungicides, killing weeds, tying up the vine fronds to form a canopy over the bunches, and so stop the great summer sun burning them. Everyone watches the skies, hoping for bright but not searing sunshine, and the occasional passing shower.

This waiting time provides an opportunity to look around the vineyards and note the grape varieties growing there. A total of 46 varieties are permitted for red and white port-making. Red port can be made from up to 27 varieties, and white port from 19. The grapes are classified into one of three groups – recommended, authorized and tolerated – and the proportion of each category planted in a vineyard will be assessed in the Register.

Many may be permitted, but few are chosen. There is a 'shortlist' of grapes, and in the future it is these varieties and these alone that will be planted and used for port production. Each variety complements others. The Mourisco, for example, bears large, high-quality grapes but without much colour, which ripen unevenly, and which are subject to *coulure* (flower abortion). Colour alone can be provided by the Sousão; and colour and quality distinguish the Tinta Barroca, the Tinta Amarella and, most importantly of all, the Touriga Nacional: perhaps the leading port variety. The Tinto Cão produces fine, complex wines – but is an unrewarding variety to grow because of its low yield (Californian development work may help in this respect). The Touriga Francesa and the Rufete both provide aroma, while the Tinta Roriz brings more colour and concentrated grape sugar to blends. Tinta Francisca or Francesca, the port grape variety traditionally but incorrectly considered a descendant of Burgundy's Pinot Noir, is sweet and perfumed, but lacks concentration. The Esgana–Cão, Folgasão, Verdelho, Rabigato, Viosinho and Malvasia Fina are the main varieties for white port.

Clonal selection (the improvement of the grape strains used) and ampelographical (grape) research in general has been comparatively neglected in the Douro. This has been reflected in the vineyards: vines were selected and planted casually, different varieties growing next to each other within a row. Even today, no port shipper will be able to say exactly what grape varieties go into his finest wine: vintage port. This is the most astonishing fact in this book. The state research centre at Quinta Santa Barbara is now working on improving standards, as is the shipper-sponsored Association for the Development of Viticulture in the Douro, and it seems likely that this will be one of the areas in which

*T*HESE ARE *two of the 46 grape varieties permitted for port production. This large number was a traditional economic safeguard: the harvest was not lost if one variety failed.*

important changes will be seen over the next two decades. Already, new plantings are much simplified. Cálem, for example, replants terraces at its Quinta da Foz with four red port varieties only: Touriga Nacional, Touriga Francesa, Tinta Roriz and Tinta Barroca. A similar picture is found at Cockburn's Vilariça development, and on quintas throughout the Douro.

The Douro vintage

Everyone who has visited the Douro at vintage time realizes that something special is happening. This is true of seasoned wine writers as much as of impressionable tourists. "Vintage time anywhere," observes Hugh Johnson in *The World Atlas of Wine*, "is the climax of the year, but in the Douro, perhaps because of the hardship of life, it is almost Dionysiac. There is an antique frenzy about the ritual, the songs, the music of drum and pipe, the long nights of treading by the light of hurricane lamps while the women and girls dance together." This Lusitanian wine harvest is one of the great seasonal moments of the old world.

At the end of August or beginning of September the shippers in Oporto pack their bags and make for the hills. Their first harvest task is to check the various farms, installations and centres where the wine is to be made, and to examine the grapes on the vines. In this as in every other aspect of the vintage, a recurring theme is the contrast, more or less plangent, between modern-day practices and those of just 20 or 30 years ago. It is as if some huge watershed was crossed about 1970, and with it the old ways became the new. There had been harbingers of the new in the 1950s and 1960s, just as vestiges of the old remain in the 1970s and 1980s, but at root everything has changed. In the old days a shipper would spend several weeks touring 'his' quintas to ensure that all was in order, ready for the wine-treading and winemaking. He would put his head into every cask, give it a hefty thump, and inhale gently to gauge its cleanliness. He would talk to the farmer, who would offer him a glass of old quinta tawny, and they would discuss the prospects for the vintage – and negotiate the likely price of the wine. The visit would finish, and the contract between the two be renewed for another year on a handshake. Nowadays the majority of farmers simply sell grapes to the shipper, who will transport them to his own wine centre where he will then make the wines himself.

There is, though, one important aspect of the vintage where past traditions are still present practices: grape-picking. It may not always be so: one day even these vineyards – or many of them – will have their grape harvesting done by machine. But for the moment things are as they have always been. The same group of harvesters, the *roga*, arrives at the quinta at the appointed time, led by the *rogador*. Accordion music greets their arrival, accompanies all their work, and will eventually serenade their departure.

Bug-killer and square meals

Mornings begin early, with a glass of *mata-bicho* (literally 'bug-killer': *bagaceira*, the local marc) for the men, and *vinho doce* (last year's wine) for the women. After several hours' work it is time for breakfast: a substantial meal of hot food with wine, followed by half-an-hours' rest. At eleven or so

more wine is issued, as it is with lunch at one – a still more substantial meal followed by an hour's rest. Thirsts are again slaked at five with more wine, enabling the workers to toil on until seven, nearly twelve hours after they began. Then comes a third square meal, with as much wine and *bagaceira* as may be required to lift spirits and limbs for the dancing that follows. Eventually, towards eleven, the accordion, triangle and drum fall quiet, and the workers make for bed – in separate quarters.

The women do most of the actual grape picking, cutting the heavy bunches from the vines with small, sharp knives or secateurs. The youngsters transfer the contents of the pickers' baskets to the much larger men's baskets, waiting between the rows. Each *cesto vindimo* contains about 60 kg (135 lb) of grapes, and the men have to walk these up or down the steep steps between the terraces: taxing work. The baskets are borne high over the back, resting on a small pillow covered by rabbit skin on the shoulders, and held in place by a thong around the forehead and a hooked, hand-held stick. Sackcloth prevents chafing; music sustains the spirit. "The effect is biblical," as Sarah Bradford has

*B*ASKETS OF grapes cut by the women (left), wait on the dry stone terrace wall for the men to porter them back to the quinta buildings.

*E*MPTY BASKETS are brought – by head, of course – back to the vineyard (above).

THE MOMENT *of the* liberadade *is greeted with delight (left); the treaders break ranks and dance freely around the* lagar. *A song is traditionally sung at this point:*
  "Liberty! Ah, Liberty!
    Only to the few you're known,
      If only I had liberty
      To call my feet my own."

noted: "nothing but the men's old grey trousers and stained check shirts has changed for over a thousand years."

The grapes arrive at the quinta. As mentioned above, grapes increasingly arrive at the wine centre rather than the quinta, and the modern winemaking process will be described in a moment. But the winemaking of the past lingers on in parts of the Alto Douro – at Taylor's Quinta de Vargellas, for example, where the company is as yet unconvinced that automated pressing and vinification can give a superior result to that obtained by traditional methods.

The grapes are tipped into a large granite trough called a *lagar*. It is about 9 m (30 ft) square, and 1.25 m (4 ft) high, and will contain enough grapes to make between 20 and 30 pipes of port. Two wine treaders are required for each final pipe.

The men, traditionally dressed in blue, link arms. They are barefoot, and wear loose briefs or shorts tucked up high, above the thigh. At the given signal, they step into the *lagar* and begin the *corte* or 'cut'. For two hours, they tread the grapes slowly and rhythmically, marching on the spot through a thick pulpy quagmire. Then comes the *liberdade*: a delirious, galumphing dance around the *lagar* to the accompaniment of accordion, triangle and drum.

THE MODERN *alternative to the granite* lagar *and the human foot is the mechanical press (right). A screw feeder transports the grapes to the crushing and stemming machine.*

Two more hours of treading follow, each man on his own now, arms crossed, reflective, exhausted. Treading grapes is, more than anything else, hard work, as hard as a four-hour barefoot wade through marshland after a day's grape-portering might be expected to be. Purple-legged, the men leave the *lagar*. The yeasts take over.

Vinification and fortification

When you buy grapes from the supermarket – or, if you are lucky, pick them from your garden or greenhouse – you will notice a dusty white bloom on them. This bloom contains yeasts. All grapes carry their own fermentation kit on their skins. After treading, the yeasts are scattered throughout the grape juice (by now known as must) and fermentation soon begins. The must grows darker, as colour is extracted from the grape skins. Soon a cap of skins, pips and pulp rises to the surface: this *manta* must be broken and refreshed by fermenting wine. Planks are run across the *lagar* and the men kneel on these, turning the wine with long spiked paddles called *macacos*. The sugar level in the must is constantly checked during this time.

Between 36 and 48 hours after fermentation commences, the right degree of sweetness is attained (on average between six and eight degrees Baumé)

and the wine is run off into a single huge cask or *tonel*. The brandy (*aguardente*) is added to the must at the same time, to stop further fermentation (one part brandy to every four of must). The air grows dreamy with the fumes. The wine is now port.

Is the human foot the best means of extracting colour and extract from grape skins, juice from pulp? Opinions are divided. It is certainly effective, thanks to its softness (the bitter pips are not crushed), warmth (aiding fermentation) and cleanliness (the washed human foot does not rust or need oiling). The method is ancient, and has worked well for centuries. It is very like walking, which is much the best method of going from one place to another, if you have the time. Long may the hand-made wines of the Douro continue to be foot-trodden.

By 'time', though, we mean 'man-time': time spent by someone doing something. This is now the most expensive of raw materials, and it is for this reason that port, most port, must have its grapes pressed and juice vinified by machine. In this respect as in so many others, the Douro is now a region of contrasts. The past is represented by the wine-scented *adega* with its brushed earth floor, granite *lagares* and roof of chestnut beams: a pleasant place to use workers' time to turn fine grapes into fine

A SMALL JUICE sample is taken when the grapes arrive at the wine centre so that the specific gravity (which indicates sugar content) of the must can be measured (left).

F ROTHING MUST wells up from the tube on the right of this autovinificator (below). When the level inside drops, carbon dioxide is released, and the must drains back into the tank.

port. At the opposite extreme, the future looks something like Sandeman's wine centre at Celeirós, where 50 autovinificators turn two million grapes into 3,500 pipes of wine every autumn. This future is as strange, beautiful and appropriate as that past, as visitors to the centre testify.

The challenge that faced the shippers several decades ago, when it was first realized that mechanized vinification was inevitable, was to find a system that would extract adequate colour, flavour and tannin from the wine during the very rapid fermentations common in the Douro. The key to this was regular pouring of the must over the *manta*. Two different machines were found that could achieve this, and both are widely used today. The first, called an autovinificator, was developed in Algeria. It is a complicated and ingenious closed-system device, rather like a coffee percolator; it makes use of the carbon dioxide given off during fermentation to provide the motor force needed to lift the must up and over the *manta*. This system is used by Sandeman, Warre, Dow and Croft among others. The other system is an open-tank alternative in which the must is simply sprayed over the *manta* by pump, with cooling of the must if conditions are very hot – as at Cockburn's installation at Foz–Côa. Quinta do Noval uses a combination of old and new:

*M*ACACOS, THE *traditional way of breaking and refreshing the* manta, *are turned by men kneeling on planks over the* lagar *(above).*

*Q*UINTA DO Bomfim's *impressive battery of autovinificators (right). The object of autovinification is to extract colour, flavour and tannin from the grape matter during a short fermentation period – as the human foot has always done.*

*D*OW'S BARCO rabelo –
*very much the dark horse
– takes an early lead in the
annual race organized by the
Confraria do Vinho do Porto.
These boats are new, but their
form is ancient: they are
thought to have been
developed by the Portuguese
from the design of the Viking
longships that travelled via
Portugal to the
Mediterranean in the 9th
century.*

the grapes are mainly pressed by machine (about 25 per cent are trodden), and they are then fermented in *lagares*, with the must being turned by men using the traditional *macacos*.

Barcos rabelos

The young ports pass their first winter up in cask in the Douro, and are moved down to Vila Nova de Gaia in the spring. (If they stay upriver over a long succession of hot summers, they acquire a special flavour, much appreciated by those that know it, called the 'Douro bake'.) Nowadays the wines are transported to the entrepôt by lorry, but in the old days they always went down river by the famous *barcos rabelos.*

Wide and flat-bottomed, these boats looked like large gondolas, with the addition of a single mast and a high wooden platform at their rear. Balanced on the boat's tapering stern was a long thin tiller (called an *espadela*) that reached the water some 6 m (20 ft) behind the boat; the other end was held by the helmsman, who stood on the wooden platform. Sails and west winds took the boats upstream. Melting snows, winter rains and oarsmen brought them downstream, loaded with up to 60

pipes of port. The Douro was a turbulent river, with many rapids and whirlpools ready to punish the unwary or complacent. These journeys were always exciting and occasionally tragic. Forrester was only the most famous of those who lost their lives while descending the river.

The new hydroelectric dams have stopped all river traffic, at least until locks are provided, but visitors to Oporto can still see *barcos rabelos* moored along the Vila Nova de Gaia waterfront, where they provide the shippers with excellent publicity. If you are lucky enough to be in Oporto on 24th June, the city's patron saint's day, you can see the *barco rabelo* race organized by the Confraria do Vinho do Porto. Most of the beautiful boats which compete are new, but these have been built from original designs with meticulous attention to detail. They make a fine sight on a breezy day.

The port lodges

In January and February, huge tankers block the elegant but impractical streets of Vila Nova de Gaia. Eighty per cent of all port is now produced in wineries: the wine is pumped direct from storage vat to tanker, and from tanker to lodge. There most of it

*T*HESE CONCRETE *storage tanks at Cockburn's Tua winery make a surreal sight (above), like a troop of giant puffballs. Their whiteness is designed to reflect light and heat, while their shape is a function of the way they are made – by spraying concrete onto a huge balloon.*

*T*HE ENTREPÔT *of Vila Nova de Gaia shouts its purpose from the rooftops – provided a few shippers' names are recognized (left). It is a town of port rather than people. If the lodges had walls of glass, thousands of pipes of port could be seen resting inside.*

*A*N AGED *tawny* lote *of 20 year-old wines in C. da Silva's Gaia lodge (right). Cleanliness, a free air flow and soft light are all essential if the wine is to mature as it should.*

*T*HE COMPLEXITY *of this Cockburn blender's task is indicated by the library of materials he has at his disposal (above).*

will be stored in wooden casks for a year or two. Some ports, particularly white ports, are stored in concrete tanks, often up in the Douro: these striking breast-shaped objects are made by spraying concrete onto a balloon.

The word 'lodge' is derived from the Portuguese word '*loja*', meaning storehouse, cellar or shop. The lodges are crowded tightly into the entrepôt – there are no less than 12 of them in one of Gaia's narrow streets – and this means congestion and noise as the wines arrive and leave. Once inside, though, all is quiet, peaceful, spacious. The lodge is where the young ports are blended and matured until ready for shipment.

The first tastings of the wines take place after the vintage in the *adegas*, up in the Douro. The ports are barely palatable at this stage, and the tasting conditions are often far from ideal. Trying to classify 30 or 40 sternly tannic wines in a cold, wet, draughty *adega* after an early breakfast is harder work than might be imagined. All the shipper can do at this stage is begin to sort the wines into different styles and quality groupings, rejecting any that are sub-standard. This initial sorting process will make subsequent work in the lodge easier. The process is known as the *lota*, and the resulting parcels of wines among which blending takes place are known as *lotes*.

On arrival at the lodge, the young ports are subjected to strict laboratory analysis. They are also retasted in ideal conditions: the light, airy, scrupulously clean, temperature-controlled lodge tasting room. After this tasting, the wines can be classified, the *lotes* definitively assembled, and blending and maturing begin.

The various types of port described in Part One of the book convey some idea of the complexities of the blender's task. There are enormous differences in taste between old tawny and young ruby, or between vintage and dated port – yet to the untrained palate many of their component wines will taste the same at six or nine months old. The blender has not only to distinguish accurately between them, but has also to foretell their development and eventual taste after five, ten, fifteen years.

Even this is only one part of the job. Once the wines have been classified into, say, a vintage or tawny *lote*, the exact blend has still to be assembled. This can be an even more complex affair, and is best illustrated by an example or two.

Chinese boxes

George Robertson (see Further Reading, page 91) describes the blending of a 10 year-old tawny carried out in 1976. Eight different wines were used from years between 1964 and 1969; two of these were already blended from wines of several years, and all would have been wines blended from different areas. The largest quantity – one third of the total blend – was of a 1965 wine; while the smallest quantity – one twenty-eighth of the whole – was a dry wine from 1964, used to counteract the sweetness of one of the younger wines in the blend. All of the wines came from the high quality Cima Corgo sector of the delimited port area.

While fine tawnies call primarily for a blend of wines of different vintages, vintage ports themselves are given balance and distinction by combining wines from different areas. As already noted, the core of a shipper's vintage port will generally be provided by the wines of that shipper's top quinta. Ben Howkins (see Further Reading, page 91) cites an example from the 1977 vintage, blended from seven different wines, the major component being the wine of Silva & Cosens's Quinta do Bomfim. (Silva & Cosens produce Dow's port.) Only two other wines in the final mix were unblended: one from another quinta near Tua, particularly successful that year; and the second – a tiny quantity – from

a small farm in the Távora valley. (Only one vat of this farm's wine was considered good enough for the vintage blend.) The remaining four wines were blended already: three were from the Rio Torto area, and one from Pinhão. Of the Torto wines, one was from the lower part of the valley, giving a wine of good concentration and moderate richness; one from the upper Torto – a light, fragrant wine; and

THE HYDROMETER confirms the palate's theory. Blending calls for scientific precision combined with artistic intuition.

the third, made at Bomfim itself, a blend of wines from small properties in all parts of the valley, giving 'a finely balanced wine, but of no pronounced character. The Pinhão wine was another light, fragrant blend, which is needed to balance the rich, dark, concentrated wine of Bomfim itself, and of the quinta near Tua.

A finished bottle of port, then, is something of a Chinese box: it is made up of blends within blends within blends. The two examples we have considered have both been high-quality wines, where variations between bottlings or years are both permissible and desirable. Most ports, though, have to be 'standard' blends, tasting the same from one year to the next, and this is a further and arguably greater test of the blender's skills.

Wood, glass and age

Blending, though, is not the only activity in a port lodge. Maturity, as most readers will be aware, is a euphemism for age, and maturation means ageing. Port is aged (or matured) in the same way as every other wine: by exposing it to air. The best way of doing this is to store wine in wooden casks, and most ports are aged for the period appropriate to their type in wooden casks in the lodges. There are

COOPERING IS still an important industry in Oporto and Gaia, as thousands of pipes are needed every year for the storage and maturation of young wine. Many lodges have their own cooperage: this is Offley Forrester's (above).

THE TASTE of new oak is not a desirable one in port, so well-seasoned casks are as valuable to the shipper as freshly coopered examples (left).

various ways of speeding up the maturation process: ageing in small casks, frequent racking (transferring the wine off its lees into a different cask, and thereby aerating it), or even leaving the wine up in the Alto Douro, where low humidity and high temperatures mean that the wine evaporates and ages quickly. There is only one way of slowing the ageing process down, which is to bottle the wine as soon as possible – as is done with vintage port.

Three things happen to most ports before they leave the lodge: clarification, stabilization and bottling. Modern technology plays an extremely important role in these operations. In the old days, ports would have been fined (clarified) with white of egg or bull's blood, perhaps filtered with a cloth bag, then bottled by hand – if at all. Most port was traditionally exported in cask, including vintage port. Such wines as were exported in bottle were never labelled: if the customer (wine merchant, college or club) wanted a label, then it would be designed and fixed to the bottle by that customer.

Nowadays, white of egg is used only occasionally, to fine very old tawnies, and bull's blood never. Gelatine is more commonly used, though this also reduces colour and tannin levels; extra tannin is often added to compensate for this loss. Another commonly used fining agent, particularly for white ports, is bentonite, a natural clay. However modern filtration systems are so effective that fining is not always necessary.

Filtration forms part of the stabilization process, in which ports are chilled to a very low temperature for anything between one hour and ten days, depending on the system used. They are then filtered cold, brought back to normal temperature, and (in the case of white port) sulphured as a final cleaning measure. Some shippers also flash-pasteurize their wines after this, before giving the wines a final series of filtrations. The main reason for this sophisticated treatment is to ensure that basic categories of port are as stable as possible: that no organism, in other words, remains in the wine to spoil its flavour. (Vintage and other high-quality ports that are to mature in bottle do not have to run this technological gauntlet.)

After all this, port is ready for the bottling line. This is another up-to-date installation in most port lodges: speed and sterility are the modern desiderata. Corks, though, deserve a special mention. Portugal is the world's largest producer of cork, and the Portuguese product is of excellent quality. Cork is the bark of the cork oak, *quercus suber*, which is periodically stripped from the tree. The third stripping is the first one that produces cork of high enough quality to stop bottles, and this not before the oak is some 35 years old. Once stripped, the bark is boiled, flattened, punched, washed again in an oxalic acid solution, dyed if necessary, and dried. It is then ready for use. All port bottles are stopped with Portuguese cork.

This, then, is the biography of port, from grape to glass. Traditionally the farmer's role has been as important as the shipper's, as it was the farmer who provided the raw material – young port – from which types and blends could be prepared in the lodges. The picture has changed somewhat of late, as only a few of the bigger farmers still make their own ports. Shippers now buy grapes to make wine in

LIKE PORT, cork is one of Portugal's national glories: the country produces over half the world's annual crop. Cork is the bark of an oak, stripped every eight years or so from the tree's fifteenth year onwards. The tree yields for up to 150 years, and bottle-quality cork is produced from year 35.

their wine centres, thus controlling most stages in the port-making chain. Cooperatives, though, are playing an increasingly important role in port production, and through partnership in these the farmers can still be port producers, selling young wines to the shippers. Thanks to the 1986 rule-change allowing shipment direct from the Douro, cooperatives have indeed begun blending, shipping and selling ports abroad directly, just as farmers in the finest areas, or those with particularly distinguished properties, have begun to produce and market their own single quinta wines abroad. But the scale on which this is occurring is as yet minute. For the time being, farmers and shippers still need each other, and will continue to do so for the foreseeable future.

Directory of port shippers

The reader is now in possession of most of the information needed to buy port knowledgeably. Only two variables remain to be discussed: the shipper's name and, where appropriate, the vintage date. Both qualitatively affect the taste of the wine. One shipper may produce characteristically rich, full-bodied wines, while another specializes in wines of delicacy and fragrance. No vintage year will ever be the same as another. The port equation is a complex one, and its solution is always expressed in a different way.

This, the final section of Part Two, will provide information on these two topics via an alphabetically ordered guide to shippers, and a vintage table. One outstanding task will then remain before an education in port is complete: tasting the wines. This will be the reader's responsibility – though Part Three will provide information on how best to set about tackling this enjoyable research.

*B*ARCOS RABELOS *on the Douro provide the shippers with their most beautiful and fitting advertisements (above).*

Andresen

A small, Portuguese-run shipping group, whose associated companies are Mackenzie (q.v.), *Pinto Pereira*, *A. P. Santos* and *Vinhos do Alto Corgo*.

Barros Almeida

One of the most important of the Portuguese shippers, not least because of its ownership of the historic port company names of Fueurheerd and Kopke (qq.v.), as well as *Santos Junior*, the *Douro Wine Shippers and Growers Association*, *Feist*, *Hutcheson* and *Vieira de Sousa*. Vintage and other quality ports are shipped, but group strength lies in medium-quality wines exported in bulk to a wide number of export markets, and in table wines. The firm was built by Manuel de Barros, who started with Almeida as an office boy. It is now run by his two sons Manuel Angelo and Joào Barros, and is the fifth largest group in Gaia.

Borges & Irmão

A large Portuguese company founded in 1884 by two entrepreneurial brothers: António and Francisco Borges. In addition to its port business, Borges & Irmão has substantial table wine interests, and makes and ships 'Lello', one of the leading Douro table wine brands.

Like many Portuguese companies, Borges & Irmão seldom used to declare vintage ports. It has, though, been declaring vintages consistently in recent years owing to ever-increasing interest in these wines, particularly from America. The company markets a full range of other ports, including 'Soalheira' and 'Roncão' tawnies in the 10 and 20 years old categories respectively; while the characterful wine of its Quinta do Junco has been one of the first dated ports to receive wide distribution in Britain. The Portuguese government are shareholders in this important employer.

Burmester

A small but historic and well-respected shipper, founded in 1730. Originally an Anglo–German partnership, the firm is now Portuguese-run, though Burmester descendants are still involved in company direction. Like Offley Forrester, Burmester suffered a tragic family loss when Johann Wilhelm Burmester, the sole owner of the company, was dragged into the sea at Foz by a giant wave on 2nd February, 1885.

Despite modest stocks, Burmester produces a wide range of ports, from vintage and LBV to good, dryish tawnies, the doyen of which is the over 40 years old 'Tordiz' *ultra reserva*. Like many of the small, non-British shippers, the company has a particularly impressive range of dated (*colheita*) ports, with vintages from 1922 onwards available in commercial quantities. *Gilberts* is a subsidiary, marketing a range of ports nearly as extensive as that of Burmester itself.

Butler Nephew

A small company founded in 1789. Having passed through Gonzalez Byass ownership, it is now the property of the Portuguese shipper *Vasconcelos Oporto*. Before World War II, Butler Nephew ports had a high reputation and sold for more than many of today's best-known names. The marque is not often seen on export markets at present.

Cálem

A prominent Portuguese shipper, founded in 1859 and today headed by one of Oporto's most indefatigable characters, Joaquim Manuel Cálem. Dr Cálem combines running the family business with directorship of the Swedish Match Company, the General Motors agency for Northern Portugal, and the Dutch Consulship in Oporto. (His relations with the Dutch government are so good that he per-

suaded them to fund the first Department of Oenology at a Portuguese university, at Vila Réal.)

Near Pinhão the company owns four linked vineyards, the most important of which is the Quinta da Foz. Here the grapes are still trodden by foot, and the wine is made by partly traditional means. Foz provides the stiffening for Cálem's elegant vintage port, whose reputation has never been better than at present. Cálem has traditionally been strong in the domestic market (its '*Velhotes*' or 'Old Friends' tawny is the biggest-seller in Portugal), as well as in France, where the **Da Costa** marque is also used. The company would like to better its position on the British and American markets, though, and the recent improvement in its vintage port, together with the release of single Quinta da Foz in secondary years, are both steps towards achieving this end. Cálem is also one of the few shippers to market an aged tawny in each of the available categories (10, 20, 30 and over 40 years old).

Churchill Graham

Founded in 1981, Churchill Graham is the first new independent port shipper to appear on the port scene in over 50 years. It is run by John Graham of the Graham port family (though he had previously worked for Cockburn and Taylor) and his wife Caroline (née Churchill), together with John's brothers William and Anthony Graham. The company is concentrating on producing top quality wines – vintage, single quinta, crusting, late-bottled vintage – originating from three properties in the upper Pinhão valley (Quintas da Tapeda, de Manuela and do Fojo), as well as from the Quinta de Água Alta on the Douro itself. Seven years is not long in the port world, but the company already enjoys an excellent reputation for intense and characterful wines, made to last and – at the moment – modestly priced.

Cockburn Smithes

One of the leading British shippers, Cockburn has the largest single share of the British market (38 per cent), and its 'Fine Ruby' and 'Special Reserve' are the two best-selling ports in Britain. At least part of the credit for this must go to its Allied Lyons stablemate Harvey, who markets all Cockburn's ports with verve and assurance.

The complete range of Cockburn ports is well respected, and since its founding in 1815 the company has led the field in many distinguished vintages (1881, 1896, 1912, 1927). At present it is always among the top ten vintage port producers, though less often in the top three. Cockburn vintage wines have the peculiarity of appearing light when young, but they age as well as any. The house style in general is dry and firm.

Fine tawny is a Cockburn strength: the 20 year-old 'Director's Reserve' is a supple, elegant and silky wine, one of the best of all branded tawnies. Cockburn also produces **Harvey's** 'Hunting' and 'Director's Bin' tawny ports.

*L*ARGE CASKS, *like this one (above) receiving attention in Cockburn's tidy lodge, are used for maturing young wines that are still throwing heavy sediment. Cask cleaning is easier from within than from without.*

Cockburn farms and buys wines and grapes from vineyards further up the Douro than any other shipper, and wines from its own quintas (Tua, Chousa and Santa Maria) are still, in part, trodden by foot. Cockburn manages and sells the wine of the Quinta da Eira Velha near Pinhão, owned by the Newman family, as a single quinta port, as well as using it in crusting port and other blends. The company also owns an extensive property at Vilariça, in the Douro's far east. This has been developed and expanded with 'Special Reserve' in mind. The vineyards are comparatively flat, making mechanization easy, and much work has gone into soil preparation, rootstock selection and block planting of grape varieties.

Cockburn has had a number of distinguished port characters in its ranks, such as Ernest Cockburn, the Grand Old Man of the London port scene between the wars, now remembered chiefly for his remark "the first duty of Port is to be red." (He was not set against white port, but against thin port.) In Portugal, Archibald and John Smithes, father and son, were thought the two greatest tasters of their times, and John was as good a spitter as taster: he could extinguish a lighted cigarette at 13 feet.

Croft

Croft is one of the oldest of all port shippers, the firm appearing on shipping lists (as Phayre and Bradley) in 1678. The first Croft entered the firm in 1736, but all returned to England during the early part of the 19th century, preferring York to Oporto. Back in York, one Croft – Percy – preferred sipping port to all other activities. "Any time not spent drinking port is a waste of time," he is remembered as philosophizing.

The Wright family succeeded the Crofts. J. R. Wright, the first of the line, lost an arm during the Portuguese Civil 'War of the Two Brothers', when a stray shell fell into his dining room as he was

enjoying a glass of fine tawny. He was known to be a man of his word: having visited the vineyards on horseback in the late summer of 1868 and found the grapes in poor condition, owing to excessive heat, he announced that Croft would make no 1868 vintage. As he left the vineyards on his return journey, though, a light rain began to fall. The grapes were harvested in perfect condition – but Croft made no 1868. (It did, though, make an excellent 1869 . . .) Gilbey bought Croft in 1911, and the company is consequently now part of the IDV (International Distillers and Vintners) group, in turn part of the Grand Metropolitan conglomerate. Robin Reid of Croft has been one of port's leading figures in the 1970s and 1980s, and is the man chiefly responsible for the Confraria do Vinho do Porto.

Croft owns the Quinta da Roêda above Pinhão, known, after some lines of the Portuguese poet Vega Cabral, as 'the Diamond of the Douro.' ("If the wine district were a golden ring, Roêda would be the diamond in that ring.") This is a very large property, and its fine, scented ports characterize Croft's

THE QUINTA da Roêda in soft spring weather. Croft is at present the owner of this historic wine-farm above Pinhão, at one time the property of Taylor's Mr Fladgate.

vintage wines. Roêda is also available as a single quinta port. Croft's leading branded tawny is 'Distinction', and the company produces a range of other port types. Its Gaia lodges are large (the Terreirinho, 136 m/149 ft long, is the largest of all), and visitors are rewarded by well-organized tours that include a film and a tasting.

Delaforce

Delaforce has been part of IDV since 1968, the shipper's centenary year. This should not obscure

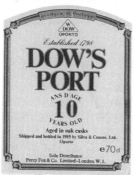

the fact that the company has been – and still is – one of the most family-orientated of all in a generally family-orientated trade. Of Huguenot origin, the first Delaforce (London-born John Flurriet Delaforce) came to Oporto to work for Martinez Gassiot (q.v.) in 1834. His second son George Henry began independent trading as Delaforce in 1868, and for 100 years the company had none but Delaforces as partners. It is still run by the fifth generation, namely David and Richard Delaforce.

The company exported wines to a large variety of markets in the 19th century, and continues to do so in the 20th; it also had the rare honour for a British shipper of being appointed a supplier to the Portuguese royal family in 1894. Delaforce produces vintage ports of delicacy and elegance – qualities generally undervalued today, particularly in America, so the wines are good value for money. It has recently entered into a long-term agreement with the Pacheco and Cyrne families to market the wines of the impeccably run Torto valley Quinta da Côrte, both as a single quinta port (beginning with the 1978 and 1980 vintages) and for use in Delaforce vintage and other ports. The company's leading brand on English-speaking markets is an old tawny, 'His Eminence's Choice', which makes a deliciously gentle starting point for those wishing to explore this style. Delaforce's 'Paramount' ruby and tawny outsell all rivals in Holland and Germany.

Dow

Dow is not the name of a shipper, but a marque owned and used by Silva & Cosens (q.v.) for vintage and other quality ports. The original 'Dow and Co.' was the firm owned by James Ramsey Dow, who became a Silva & Cosens partner in 1877. Mr Dow's character is illustrated by the story of a sales trip he made to Manchester to see a wine merchant who had been out of the office (he had been told) on each of the several previous occasions when he had called. This time he saw the man at his desk as he approached the building – but was again told he was out. Enough was enough. Mr Dow's gaze fixed on the key in the office door behind which the recalcitrant merchant sheltered. He quietly turned it and pocketed it, and then tossed it in the Manchester Canal as he left. On his next visit he was received by the merchant, who became a faithful customer.

Dow's port is known for, and advertises itself with, its dry style. The Quinta do Bomfim at Pinhão provides a sizeable proportion of the wine for its deep, dark vintage ports. Bomfim is soon to be

A BARRAGE *of mist lingers theatrically on the Douro (left). The high terraces of Dow's Quinta do Bomfim escape its chilly embrace and enjoy the morning sunshine instead.*

released as a single Quinta wine; and it has always provided stiffening for Dow's excellent crusted, late-bottled vintage and vintage character offerings. Bomfim itelf houses one of the largest wine-making *adegas* in the Douro, which acts as a centre of operations for the Symington group (see Silva & Cosens, Warre), at vintage time. The Dow range of tawnies includes lively 10, 20 and 30 year olds, as well as Dow's Boardroom, a 'Finest Old' blend characterized by a tangy aroma and fruity flavour with a complex, dry finish.

Ferreira

Historically the most important of all the Portuguese shippers, Ferreira is still held in great esteem and affection by all port shippers and port enthusiasts. The company, founded in 1751 and now owned by Mateus Rosé/Sogrape, is closely associated with the memory of Dona Antónia Ferreira (1811–1896), the immensely wealthy, twice-widowed *grande dame* of 19th-century port, that same lady whose crinoline saved her from the swirling Douro waters that claimed Baron Forrester's life (see page 36–7). The company achieved its greatness under her guidance, and her shade oversees its present-day progress. Two superb quintas – Quinta do Vesúvio and Quinta do Vale de Meão, both high up the Douro – belong to Ferreira. "Imagine, if you can, a vineyard containing within its walls, seven hills and thirty valleys!" So wrote Charles Sellers of Vesúvio, perhaps the largest and grandest of all Douro quintas. Ferreira owns eight properties in all (the other six are Quintas das Nogueiras, do Valado, do Porto, do Seixo, Do Porrais and da Leda), and these provide nearly 40 per cent of its ports: the highest percentage of this sort in the trade.

The company is particularly well-known for its tawnies. Top of the range is the nutty, succulent 20 years old Duque de Bragança, produced largely from wines from the Quinta do Roriz, owned by the van Zeller family (see Kopke, Gonzalez Byass, Quinta do Noval); a fine 10 years old single quinta tawny, Quinta do Porto, is also marketed. Ferreira vintage ports are rich, fruity, sweet, soft, luscious: not to the traditional British taste, but often superb in their own comely way, and somewhat undervalued. The company has a library of these in which every vintage from 1815 to the present is represented.

The firm is also known by the diminutive form Ferreirinha (acquired, like so much else, by Dona

*F*ERREIRA'S IMPOSING *Quinta do Vesúvio. This, one of the region's largest estates, is situated just west of Pocinho, in the severe, remote and parched high Douro.*

Antónia), and this serves as a brand name for one of its excellent Douro table wines (which, to confuse matters further, is known as Barca Velha in the very best years). Ferreirinha is made at Quinta do Meão. Another good Ferreira table wine – Esteva – is made at Quinta do Seixo. The company symbol is, obscurely, an emu. Hunt Roope (q.v.) and **Constantino** are subsidiaries.

Fonseca Guimaraens

Guimaraens was, until 1988, the name of the shipping company producing and marketing Fonseca ports. The company is now simply known as Fonseca Giumaraens Vinhos.

The first Guimaraens, Manuel Pedro, acquired Fonseca Monteiro in 1822, and decided at that time to use the name Fonseca alone for the wines because of its easy pronunciation and the fact that it was already known to customers. Manuel Pedro settled in England, married an English woman, became a well-known botanist, and had three sons, English in all but name; so it is that Fonseca Guimaraens is considered an English family business. It is still family-run, by Bruce Guimaraens, although it has been owned by the Yeatman family of Taylor, Fladgate and Yeatman (q.v.) since 1948.

Fonseca has a distinguished reputation, in particular for its statuesque vintage wines. These are always near the top in blind tastings, and are as good today as at any time previously. Vintages are founded on wines from Fonseca's two Val de Mendiz quintas: do Cruziero and Santo Antonio, at both of which a proportion of the grapes are still trodden. A 'single quinta' port christened 'Fonseca Guimaraens' has been marketed on a number of occasions, and Quinto do Cruzeiro is to be released on this basis in the future. Fonseca's 'Bin 27' is a toothsome young port. The company's tawnies are less well known, but a source of great pride to their makers. This is a marque that rarely disappoints.

Fueurheerd

A small but historic shipper, founded in 1815 by a young German, Diedrich Fueurheerd. The company is now the property of Barros Almeida (q.v.). The Fueurheerds were known for their ownership of the lovely Quinta la Rosa (see Rebello Valente), and this has remained in the family – latterly called Bergqvist – despite the sale of the marque. Barros Almeida continues to ship Fueurheerd vintage ports.

Gonzalez Byass

The famous sherry house maintained a port-shipping presence from 1896 until 1983. Its heyday was during the first three decades of this century, when it had an arrangement with the van Zeller family to ship the wines of Quinta do Roriz, which it did – as vintage port, under the Quinta Roriz label.

Gould Campbell

Another small but long-established British shipper, founded in 1797 and now one of the portfolio of companies owned and managed by the Symington family (see Warre). The Gould Campbell name is mainly used for vintage ports, which have a low market profile but high standing among connoisseurs. Hugh Johnson describes them as "big, dark, powerful and very long-lasting"; others find them delicate and intensely fruity ports. The wines of the Quinta dos Lagares above Pinhão provide a sizeable proportion of the final vintage blend. Gould Campbell also produces ruby and vintage character ports, but no LBV or aged tawnies. The wines are bottled and shipped under the aegis of Smith Woodhouse (q.v.).

*G*RAHAM'S QUINTA *dos Malvedos. Due to the steepness of the hillsides, the terraces are comparatively narrow and can therefore take only two rows of vines.*

Graham

Graham is one of the most famous British port names. It is particularly appreciated for its vintage wines and its 'Malvedos': a single quinta-type wine made in secondary years, based on ports produced at the company's Quinta dos Malvedos below Tua. The firm was founded in Lisbon as a textile business in 1808, and only began shipping port by accident, after accepting 27 pipes in settlement of a bad debt. The bad debt rapidly came good, selling for more than its cash equivalent after shipment to Scotland, and in 1822 an Oporto office was opened for trading in wine. The Scottish connection remained strong over the years, and the company has always kept offices in Glasgow. Graham has until recently been a family-run concern, but in 1970 the firm was acquired by the Symington group (see Warre), and James Symington is now in charge.

Graham's vintage ports are regularly among the most attractive of each year's declared offerings: rich, fat, creamy wines of great sweetness, often with a chocolate flavour to them. Malvedos shares these

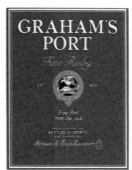

characteristics, but because it is released in lesser years it is necessarily a lighter wine. The fruit at Malvedos itself is still partially trodden, and gives wines noted for their ripeness. The Symingtons are in the process of increasing production at Malvedos from the 55 pipes produced each year when they acquired the quinta to some 350 annually.

Graham's late-bottled vintage ports are generally most successful, following the sumptuous house style, and the company has recently relaunched its 'Six Grapes' brand. This name does not refer to the wine's origins or constituents, but was a company mark from the days when ports were exclusively sold in this way (see page 17). 'Six Grapes' is one of the top-quality young ports competing on its own terms with other shippers' vintage character wines. Tawnies (in the 10, 20 and 30 years old categories) are also released, though these fare less well than others of the Graham ilk in comparative tastings.

Gran Cruz

Visitors to France may well come across 'Porto Cruz', the biggest selling brand in the world's leading port-consuming country. This is the product of an independent Portuguese company which until recently held no stocks of its own, instead buying what it needed as and when necessary from other shippers: a strategy that proved extremely profitable for it.

Hunt Roope

Founded in 1735, this is another small British company with a distinguished history: its Newman members had already been trading dried cod and wine between Portugal and Newfoundland up to a century prior to this date. The most famous partner was Cabel Roope (see page 90), and he acquired the Quinta da Eira Velha for the firm (see Cockburn). This is now owned by the Newman family, while Hunt Roope itself has belonged to Ferreira (q.v.) since 1956. *Tuke Holdsworth* is a name used by Hunt Roope for vintage ports.

Kopke

In 1636 the Hanseatic Free Towns sent Nicholas Kopke to Oporto as Consul. He must have found commercial life there promising, for two years later his son Christiano arrived and set himself up as a general/wine merchant. So began C. N. Kopke & Co., the oldest of all port shippers.

The Kopkes became a distinguished Oporto family, one member – Nicolau – having sufficient

influence with Pombal to be able to persuade him to allow the firm to export vintage Quinta do Roriz, which at that time lay outside the delimited zone. The last direct descendant, Joaquim, died in 1895.

The marque has belonged to Barros Almeida (q.v.) since 1952, and Kopke vintage port is still shipped, as single Quinta São Luiz. Quinta do Roriz is in van Zeller ownership, its wines being sold to Ferreira (q.v.) for old tawny purposes – though it is likely that in the future Roriz will be marketed as a single quinta vintage wine.

Mackenzie

A small company founded during the 19th century by Kenneth Mackenzie, a sherry shipper. The firm always enjoyed an excellent reputation, but the squeeze on small shippers after World War II necessitated its sale, and Andresen (q.v.) acquired the company. The new owners have kept the marque alive, and in 1982 a Mackenzie vintage was again shipped, the first for 16 years.

Martinez Gassiot

This port-shipping firm was founded in London in 1790 by a Spaniard, Sebastian Gonzalez Martinez, who sold port, sherry and Havana cigars. He was joined in 1822 by John Peter Gassiot, a distinguished scientist, friend of Faraday, and sometime vice-president of the Royal Society. The company was extremely successful during the 19th century, and shipped more port and sherry to Britain in the 1850s than any other concern. Throughout this period and the first half of the 20th century, it shipped in bulk, as did its arch-rivals Cockburn. Names on bottles would always have been those of its customers, rather than its own. This left the company with little or no 'market image', at a time when such things were becoming more and more important. Ironically Martinez Gassiot and Cockburn are now stablemates, John Harvey hav-

ing acquired them both in the early 1960s. While Cockburn (q.v.) has been groomed into British market leadership by Harvey, Martinez Gassiot plays a more modest role, specializing in 'own-brand' sales, quality tawnies (like Cockburn, it markets an excellent 20 years old 'Directors') and – most interestingly – some good crusting ports. The company has a stake in Cockburn's Vilariça development.

Messias

Sociedade Agrícola e Comercial dos Vinhos Messias, to give the firm its full name, is an ambitious, family-run Portuguese shipper of comparative youth (founded 1926). The company has built up extensive vineyard holdings of 290 ha (717 acres) in the Douro, including the Quinta do Cachão, where the grapes for vintage and other high-quality ports are trodden in traditional style, and the Quinta do Rei. Messias ports are sold in distinctive high-shouldered bottles. **Alberto de Castro Lança** is a subsidiary company.

Morgan

Morgan was founded in 1715 by a Mr Haughton of Clerkenwell in London. The company acquired its present name only at the end of the century, when Aaron Morgan became a partner, having joined the business some years earlier as a clerk. The firm's chief claim to fame is the fact that one of its brands, Dixon's 'Double Diamond', is mentioned in *Nicholas Nickelby*. "A magnum of the Double Diamond, David; to drink the health of Mr Linkinwater . . . ." Croft, who acquired Morgan in 1952, is said to be considering relaunching Dixon's Double Diamond.

Niepoort

A small shipper of Dutch origin, founded in 1842. It is still family-run, by Rolf van der Niepoort and his son Dirk. The Niepoort range is extensive, and of high quality: specialities include vintage, dated (*colheita*) and *garrafeira* ports, as well as tawnies in the 10, 20 and 30 years old categories. The company has an astonishing library of old *colheita* and *garrafeira* ports, the latter being aged in wood for about five years, before being run into glass demi-johns, where the wine remains for 30 or 40 years. It is then decanted into normal bottles before sale. These are elegant, aromatic ports for the collector.

Offley Forrester

A firm founded in 1761, whose present name joins that of an old City of London family (Sir Thomas Offley was Lord Mayor in 1556), no members of which ever lived in Oporto, to that of Joseph James Forrester, the most gifted and charismatic man the port trade ever produced, who lived and died on the Douro. Nowadays the company is chiefly associated with the Quinta da Boa Vista, situated downriver from Pinhão: Offley Forrester vintages are sold as 'Offley Boa Vista', and are almost exclusively the product of the vineyards at Boa Vista. Boa Vista LBVs are also produced. The company additionally owns the Quinta do Cachucha, where it produces an intriguing single quinta wood-aged white port. It has in total about 81 ha (200 acres) of its own vineyards.

The rest of the Offley range includes excellent 10 years old, 20 years old and dated tawnies, sold under the 'Baron de Forrester' name and featuring a portrait of Joseph James on the label, as well as 'Duke of Oporto' ruby and tawny.

Offley Forrester became part of the Sandeman (q.v.) group in 1962; Sandeman then sold fifty per cent of the company and its subsidiaries **Diez Hermanos** and **Rodrigues Pinho** to the French St Raphaël concern in 1965. Since then the company has been wholly acquired by Martini & Rossi, itself owned by the Swiss company General Beverage.

Poças Junior

Manoel D. Poças Junior is this shipper's full name. Founded in 1918, it is another of the 'new' generation of Portuguese shippers hungry for a measure of parity on the quality export markets provided by English-speaking countries. The company has already done very well on the French and Belgian markets, winning a government export award for sales doubled there in the early 1980s. Poças owns two traditionally-run quintas in the Douro – das Quartas and Santa Barbara – and has been declaring vintages since the mid-1960s.

Quarles Harris

Quarles Harris is a further small British marque of distinguished ancestry: the firm was founded in 1680, and is therefore one of the oldest of all. It became part of Warre (q.v.) by marriage rather than takeover, and thus is today another arrow in the Symington quiver.

Quarles Harris (the Quarles is pronounced to rhyme with 'squalls') possesses no vineyards of its own: most of the wine for its ports comes from long-established contacts with grape farmers in the Rio Torto area. Quarles Harris vintages vary more than most. In good years they can be well-structured, chunky wines; at other times they are either coarse, or light and rather dull. They are modestly priced, though, and can offer good value if chosen with care. The rest of the range is sold under the 'Harris' brand (no Quarles), and includes a good 20 years old tawny, as well as crusting and LBV ports. Regrettably, perhaps, the company's 'Invalid Port' is no longer marketed. This old brand was said to contain "many valuable health-promoting properties," and was "repeatedly prescribed by Medical Practitioners to all sufferers from anaemia and kindred complaints."

Quinta do Côtto

This quinta, owned by the Montez Champalimaud family, is a producer of Douro table wines and ports of the new 'single vineyard, estate bottled' variety. The property, situated near Régua, comprises 110 ha (272 acres) of which just under half are vineyards, so the quantities produced are modest. Both the table wine and port are made from the same blend of grape varieties: Tinta Roriz, Tourigas Francesa and Nacional, and Tinto Cão. The estate is run with crusading zeal by Miguel Champalimaud, and the first vintages to appear abroad have greatly impressed tasters.

The French name 'Champalimaud' entered the family several centuries ago, when one of the granddaughters of Joseph Champalimaud – a general from Limoges who had fled France during the Revolution – married António de Aranjo Cabral Montez, the Morgado (eldest son and heir) of Cidadelhe. The children assumed both parents' surnames, a common Portuguese and Spanish practice.

TERESA VAN Zeller, who runs Quinta do Noval in partnership with her brother Cristiano, stands on a terrace with Manuel, one of Noval's vineyard workers.

Quinta do Noval

This firm, founded in 1813, was until 1973 known as A. J. da Silva. For many years, the company's energies have been directed towards the perfection of its magnificent wine farm above Pinhão, and all da Silva vintages shipped since 1908 have been single Quinta do Noval wines, and so named. Confusion with another Portuguese shipper, C. da Silva (q.v.), was still felt to cost the firm trade, hence the recent change of name for all of its range. It is important to remember, though, that it is only the vintage wine which is a true single quinta port: the rest of the range is blended from the produce of a number of scattered vineyards.

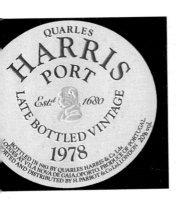

Of all Portuguese shippers, Quinta do Noval enjoys perhaps the best reputation for its vintage wines abroad, which always command top prices at auction in London. Especially venerated are its 'Nacional' wines, made from a small plot of ungrafted (hence 'pre-phylloxera') vines. Anyone who is interested in what the great 19th century vintages might have tasted like should try and sample some Noval Nacional, though it will not be easy: the company does not sell it (only 250 cases are made each year), and it appears rarely at auction. The wine is darker in colour than even the most concentrated of its rivals, and takes longer to mature. When finally ready (and the 1947, for example, is still some years off full maturity) the port is muscular, sinewy and concentrated, with an intense perfume that suggests raspberries, blackcurrants and violets. 'Ordinary' Noval vintages of the 1920s and 1930s are also collector's items, in particular 1927 and 1931. The latter was a great year declared, because of uncertain market conditions, by few shippers, and of these Noval is the finest by a considerable margin: "the Everest of Vintage Port," noted Michael Broadbent on tasting it in October 1981. "Unready – 50 years of life ahead!" Nacional '31 holds the port auction record for a single bottle of £1,250, and is, according to Cristiano van Zeller (see below), more deeply coloured, even today, than any subsequent vintage save 1985.

Recent Noval vintages seem rather lighter and softer than their fabulous ancestors, while still being wines of great finesse and rich fruit flavour. This may be misleading: Noval's vintage ports tend to age far better than their early accessibility and softness suggests to the British palate. The company's best-selling port is its rounded and liquorous 'LB', and it produces a characterful range of old tawnies, including a fine 'over 40 years old'.

In recent years, the company's centre of gravity has switched to the quinta, following a catastrophic fire in its Gaia lodge in 1981. Quinta do Noval is now run with great enthusiasm, dedication and charm by the young brother-and-sister team of Cristiano and Teresa van Zeller. The property itself, with its 'Cathedral' (a vast lodge, completed in 1985) and vineyards may now be visited, by appointment with the Oporto office: an opportunity not to be missed if you are in the region. *Osborne* is a subsidiary.

Ramos–Pinto

Adriano Ramos–Pinto is another leading Portuguese port-shipper. The company was founded in 1880 by Adriano Ramos–Pinto, then just over 20 years old. Today it owns the larger half of the divided Rio Torto Quinta do Bom–Retiro, as well as Quintas San Domingos, da Ervamoira and da Urtiga.

Ramos–Pinto has traditionally specialized in the Brazilian market, where it remains the best-seller, but it is now the second biggest shipper in Switzerland and has impressive sales across the rest of Europe. The company's vintage ports have been on sale in Britain and the USA, but its strength lies in much-admired tawnies, those of Bom–Retiro being used for a 20 years old, and from Ervamoira for a 10 years old. Quinta da Urtiga produces Ramos–Pinto vintage character port. The company also has available some very old dated (*colheita*) ports, including a vaunted 1937.

Adriano Ramos–Pinto, the 'Portuguese Maecenas', was a great patron of the arts. His fin-de-siècle tastes are reflected in the superb collection of posters owned by the company, several examples of which may be seen in this book. Many more may be seen in a visit to its waterfront lodge in Gaia.

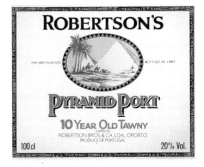
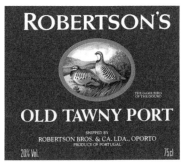

Real Companhia Vinícola do Norte de Portugal

This is the full name of what is at present the largest port producer in Vila Nova de Gaia. The company has an enormous lodge, part of which is formed by an old railway tunnel. Stocks of vintage port are stored in this, and the company has bottles from every declared year since 1765, thanks to its acquisition of the Companhia Velha (see below). There are also 14,000 pipes of port in the lodge, 20 stainless steel tanks of 2,000-pipe capacity each, six bottling lines, and huge stocks of table wine and sparkling wine. The concern has been built up by Senhor da Silva Reis, described by Wyndham Fletcher (see Further Reading, page 91) as a "meteoric tycoon". After the revolution of 1974 it became a worker's cooperative and the da Silva Reis family moved abroad, but it returned to private ownership in 1978. The full name of this company is generally shortened to Real Vinícola.

Confusion still arises over names, however, due to the fact that after World War II Real Vinícola absorbed the shipping descendant of Pombal's original monopoly company (see pages 20–21), whose full name was the Companhia Geral da Agricultura dos Vinhos do Alto Douro, in turn generally referred to as the Companhia Velha. This company ships ports to English markets as The Royal Oporto Wine Company. You will sometimes see the business as a whole referred to as the Real Companhia Vinícola Group, or the Real Companhia Velha. Seven names: one firm.

The company owns eight Douro quintas including das Carvalhas and do Sibio, and both of these are now shipped as single quinta ports, together with a full range of other ports including Royal Oporto vintage and tawnies. These are enjoyable wines, sometimes slightly rustic in character and developing with comparative speed in bottle (all but the sternest vintages would be ready within ten years). The Real Vinícola lodge is well-worth visiting for its size and scale. It will be still more attractive to the visitor when the company completes its wine museum, based on the documentary treasures that came into its possession with the Companhia Velha. **Richard Hooper** and **Silva Reis** are subsidiaries of Real Vinícola.

Rebello Valente

A marque originally owned by Allen and Co., but in the possession of Robertson (see below) since June 1881, and used exclusively for distinguished vintage port. Rebello Valente vintages are based largely on grapes grown and trodden at the lovely Quinta la Rosa near Pinhão (see Fueurheerd), and are known for their finely judged balance of sweetness, richness and fruitiness.

Robertson

Robertson Brothers, owners of Rebello Valente (see above), have themselves been owned by Sandeman (q.v.) since 1953. The company had always been associated with the Quinta do Roncão, but this was not included in the sale to Sandeman.

Robertson's speciality is its excellent tawny range, much appreciated by this style's enthusiasts: the five year-old 'Privateer', the 10 years old 'Pyramid', and the 20 years old 'Imperial'. Back labels provide plausible explanations for these intriguing names.

Royal Oporto Wine Company

see Real Companhia Vinícola do Norte de Portugal

Rozés

The port-producing sector of this French company is a joint venture between its owners Moët–Hennessy and Taylor (q.v.). Rozés specializes in producing ruby, tawny and white ports for the French market, though recently the company has begun declaring vintages, too.

Sandeman

Sandeman has always been a forward-looking company, sharing the vigorous commercial optimism of its founder, George Sandeman.

> It is but lately that I have taken up this project of growing rich, but I find it has been of infinite service to me already. One may see the marks of thriving on my face. I eat like a man for a wager. People stand out of my way as they see me bustling along the streets. I have a good word to say to everybody I meet, and, as I am informed laugh in my sleep.

So George wrote to his sister Jean in May 1790. In November of that year, his optimism unabated, he borrowed £300 from his father and brother to rent a wine vault in the City of London. He was soon shipping port and then sherry into the country, with Madeira following a little later. Business prospered; George travelled to and from Spain and Portugal.

He became a friend of Wellington's during the Peninsula War. Towards the end of his life, back in London, he became known as 'Old Cauliflower' thanks to the venerable white wig he still wore to do business. The firm has always been family-run, in the main from London rather than Oporto, and continues to be family-run to this day, despite its sale

to Seagram in 1980. David Sandeman is Chairman of Geo. G. Sandeman Sons & Co. Ltd., and his brother Timothy Sandeman is Chairman of Seagram (UK).

Sandeman prescience meant that it was the first British port shipper to advertise its name and to sell wine direct to the customer in its own labelled bottles, beginning in 1922. By 1928 the Don – the company's trademark – had made an appearance, the first of many. The original drawing was the work of George Massiot Brown, and the figure neatly sums up Sandeman's interests, having donned the traditional Portuguese student's cape as well as the wide-brimmed hat affected by the *caballeros* (horseriders) of Jerez.

Strangely enough the company owned no vineyards of its own until 1974. Since then it has acquired the Pinhão Quintas de Confradeiro and de Celeirós, and has developed the Quinta das Laranjeiras, high up the Douro near the Spanish border. Its substantial grape purchases are vinified at four Douro wine centres: Pacheca, Celeirós, Riba Tua and Pocinho, and these may be visited by appointment through Sandeman London or Oporto.

Sandeman vintage ports at present seem to lack the glamour of auction leaders like Taylor, Graham or Warre. Nevertheless they are of high quality, with deep minty fruit, concentration and length, and a dryish finish. Perhaps its excellent 1985 marks a return to top form. The rest of the range is of enviable consistency, with some particularly good LBVs and tawnies.

C. da Silva

This small, Spanish-run shipper produces vintage, LBV, tawny and white ports under the ***Presidential*** and ***Dalva*** names, as well as that of da Silva itself. Most of the fruit is bought from growers with whom firm links have been established over the firm's 100

*S*ANDEMAN'S INESCAPABLE *Don (above) – seen here surmounting the company's Gaia lodge – was offered speculatively to the advertising manager, E. Marshall Hardy, in 1928. He bought the drawing on the spot for 50 guineas.*

years of existence. Da Silva also has a wide range of dated (*colheita*) ports in stock in Oporto: vintages for these stretch back to the 1930s, and the wines are only bottled to order.

Silva & Cosens

Silva & Cosens, a firm founded in 1862 by J. J. da Silva, was merged in 1877 with Dow & Co., and all its ports are sold under the Dow (q.v.) name. The firm amalgamated with Warre (q.v.) in 1912, and is thus a cornerstone of the Symington family group (which also includes Graham, Smith Woodhouse, Gould Campbell and Quarles Harris, qq.v.).

Smith Woodhouse

This small but esteemed shipper was founded in 1784 by Christopher Smith, who later became a Member of Parliament and Lord Mayor of London. William, James and Robert Woodhouse joined the company in the early 19th century, and it became Smith Woodhouse Bros. & Co. in 1828. Graham (q.v.) began to ship Smith Woodhouse ports in 1956, and acquired the marque in full in the 1960s. Through Graham, the company has passed into Symington control – though Smith Woodhouse, like all of their marques, is run very much as an individual concern.

Smith Woodhouse vintage ports enjoyed a first-class reputation during the latter half of the 19th century, Saintsbury considering this shipper's 1887 ('the Jubilee') the best of the year. Today the company's vintage ports perform well in blind tastings, though often selling at prices some 20 per cent below wines they nearly equal in quality. They are based on fruit from the Quinta do Vale de Dona Maria in the Rio Torto valley and from the Quinta do Monte Bravo, where the crop is still trodden. Smith Woodhouse may release Dona Maria's wine as a single quinta port in the future. The firm produces excellent crusted and late-bottled vintage wines, among the best of all: both deserve at least

five year's bottle age. It also produces one of the best of the 'light' (17°) dry white ports. The house style is soft, fragrant and full of charm.

Taylor, Fladgate and Yeatman

This is the port-shipping company of which it is customary to use only superlatives. Taylor's vintage ports command the highest prices at auction almost automatically, and justify these by drawing eulogies from trade professionals and wine critics at blind tastings. The company's single Quinta de Vargellas vintages are no less successful, no less admired. (The 1947 is still drinking well.) In a blind tasting of aged tawnies conducted by *Decanter* magazine in 1984, it was Taylor's 20 years old that took top honours. Taylor pioneered the modern LBV style, and its own LBVs have been an enormous commercial success – deservedly so. Can the company do nothing wrong?

Well, not even Taylor has been able to give the 'own-brand' vintage character it has supplied to supermarkets and wine merchants much character,

TAYLOR'S SHOWPIECE, the Quinta de Vargellas. The elegant painted lettering is the work of the local stationmaster.

let alone of the vintage sort; while early tastings suggest that the company's 1985 vintage may have been bettered by Graham, Warre and its own Fonseca among others. It was Taylor that confused the trade and customers alike by bringing out both a vintage and an LBV wine in 1983. But these are scarcely failings. The fact remains that this independent company, still owned and run by Yeatman relatives, is the yardstick by which all others are judged.

Its founder was Mr Job Bearsley of Viana, a 'red Portugal' pioneer. His company was registered in 1692. He had five sons, and it was one of these – Peter – who was the first Englishman to visit the Upper Douro on a wine-buying expedition. Another son, Bartholemew, was the first English purchaser of a Douro property, the Casa dos Alembiques near Régua, which still remains in Taylor's ownership today. By rights 'Bearsley'

should feature in the company name, but this went through no less than 21 changes between 1692 and 1844, when it assumed its present form: the Bearsleys disappear from the records in 1806. Between 1808 and 1813 the name Camo appears: this belonged to the only American ever taken into partnership in a port company. He was described by a contemporary as "a typical American, full of energy, fertile in resource and never wanting in pluck." All of these qualities served his company well during the Napoleonic siege years of 1807–11, when the British had to leave Oporto while he, as a neutral, stayed on. Joseph Taylor came into partnership in 1816, John Fladgate in 1837, and Morgan Yeatman in 1844.

Taylor bought the Quinta de Vargellas (above São João da Pesqueira) in 1893, after the depradations of the phylloxera years. At this time the farm was badly run down, and produced barely six pipes of port a year. Nowadays, following decades of patient restoration, output is about 150 pipes a year, all of it trodden by foot. In recent years, Taylor has also bought and systematically replanted the Quinta de Terra Feita in the Pinhão valley, and this is to be offered in the future as a single quinta wine to complement Vargellas, beginning with the 1976 vintage. Another new Taylor venture is the release of its 'First Estate: Lugar das Lages' port. Lugar das Lages ('the place of the stepping stones') is an alternative name for the Casa dos Alembiques, and its choice for the label of this top quality non-dated port indicates the wine's importance for Taylor (but not, one should note, its provenance). 'First Estate', with its tea-caddy fragrance and velvety fruit, seems set to be another Taylor triumph. For the sake of completeness, it should be noted that Taylor owned the Quinta da Roêda (see Croft) throughout the second half of the 19th century. Fonseca, Guimaraens, Rozés and *Vinícola do Choupelo* are all subsidiaries.

Taylor is often referred to as 'the Latour of

Warre

This company was founded in or about 1670, making it the oldest of all the British shippers. The first Warre came into the business in 1729; paradoxically, though, the most famous member of the family, William Warre, is chiefly known for his manner of leaving the trade – at an early age. One hot and tedious afternoon in Oporto, the young William, who contrary to family wishes wanted a military career, fixed the pigtail of a napping Portuguese member of the firm to his desk with sealing wax. William then left the office. This prank, and the storm that followed it, ensured that his career wishes were granted. He later rose to the rank of lieutenant–general. His sister, meanwhile, became a nun.

*T*HE WASHING dries and the grapes ripen at Warre's Quinta da Cavadinha. During very hot summers, clouds like these can be a welcome sight in the Douro, particularly if they bring a little refreshing rain.

The first member of the Symingtons (undoubtedly the most important British family in Oporto at present) came into partnership initially with Warre, so perhaps it would be appropriate to give an account of their rise to eminence here. This first member was Andrew James Symington, who had begun his career in the cotton cloth side of Graham in 1882, at the age of nineteen. He quickly moved to the wine side of the firm, and from there was offered managership of Southard's. In 1905 he was invited

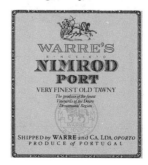

ports'. The comparison with that Bordeaux château and its massive, imposing wines – wines that in maturity typify the best that the region has to offer – is in every way appropriate.

to become a Warre partner, and when Silva & Cosens amalgamated with Warre in 1912, he took over the running, in Oporto, of both firms. His sons Maurice, John and Ronald joined him over the next decade, and in time the family came into complete ownership of both Silva & Cosens and Warre. This gave them the Dow, Warre and Quarles Harris marques, to which they have added Graham with Smith Woodhouse, and Gould Campbell more recently. The group, at present run by Michael (Maurice's son, soon to retire), Ian (John's son) and James (Ronald's son) has stocks of some 65,000 pipes, making the combined operation (on paper: in practice each company is run separately) the trade's second biggest. With more sons waiting to join the company, the future for the Symingtons, and their marques, looks extremely bright.

Warre vintage ports have always been among the best of any widely declared year and, like its stablemates, Warre is in a particularly healthy state at the time of writing. The house style is magisterial, with generous fruit and tannin alike. Warre vintages are based on wine from the Serôdio family's part of the divided Quinta do Bom–Retiro and Warre's own Quinta da Cavadinha, where the grapes are not trodden but mechanically crushed and the wines made by autovinification, as at Dow's Quinta do Bomfim. Traditional methods are not the only way of producing ports of excellence. Cavadinha, situated above Pinhão and a comparatively recent acquisition, is to be offered as a late-release single quinta wine, beginning with the 1978 vintage.

Warre's 'traditional' LBVs and crusting ports are both excellent, sturdy wines that improve with keeping. The LBV, in particular, is a very fine wine, being bottled at four years and given further maturation and 'crusting time' in the Gaia lodge before being released. The firm's 'Nimrod' is a reliable tawny. Warre has important French sales under the Cintra label, and in recognition of this has taken its French agents Dubonnet–Cinzano–Byrrh into partnership.

Wiese & Krohn

A medium-sized, independent company founded by two Germans, Theodore Wiese and Dankert Krohn, in 1865, and now Portuguese-run. Wiese & Krohn owns no vineyards of its own, but produces a full range of wines including vintage ports, dated (*colheita*) ports and a Rio Torto vintage character wine, all of which are shipped to a large number of export markets.

Who owns what?

This table shows the pattern of ownership among port shippers. The number beside each company or group indicates its relative size in terms of the number of pipes of wine sold in 1986

Andresen 20
Mackenzie
Pinto Pereira
A. P. Santos
Vinhos do Alto Corgo

Barros Almeida 5
Douro Wine Shippers
 and Growers
Feist
Feuerheerd
Hutcheson
Kopke
Santos Junior
Vieira de Sousa

Borges & Irmão 14

Burmester 21
Gilberts

Cálem 12
da Costa Oliveira

Churchill Graham 23

**Cockburn Smithes
(Allied Lyons) 4**
Martinez Gassiot

Croft (IDV) 9
Delaforce
Morgan

Ferreira 11
Constantino
Hunt Roope
Tuke Holdsworth

Gran Cruz 6

Messias 15
de Castro Lança

Niepoort 22

**Offley Forrester (Martini &
Rossi) 7**
Diez Hermanos
Rodrigues Pinho

Poças Junior 13

Quinta do Noval 19
Osborne

Ramos–Pinto 18
Carvalho Macedo

Real Vinicola 1
Companhia Velha/Royal
 Oporto
Richard Hooper
Silva Reis

Sandeman (Seagram) 3
Robertson
Rebello Valente
Sarano

C. da Silva 17

Taylor 8
Fonseca Guimaraens
Rozés
Vinicola de Choupelo

Vasconcelos Oporto 10
Butler Nephew

Warre (Symington group) 2
Gould Campbell
Graham
Quarles Harris
Silva & Cosens (Dow)
Smith Woodhouse

Wiese & Krohn 16

Port vintages

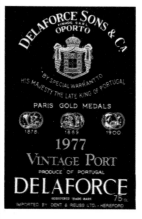

Vintages should not be a cause of anxiety to the port buyer, for wines made during poor years (the avoidance of which is normally the reason for studying vintage charts) will not appear on the market at all. They will be used for blending with other wines from better years, and will eventually emerge as standard non-vintage ruby or tawny ports. The only major vintage distinction is between wines from average-to-good years, and those from good-to-excellent years; this distinction is already drawn for the purchaser by the sort of wine on offer (see pages 24–31). In discussing the merits of declared vintages, then, as is done below, we are differentiating between various sorts of excellence. In principle at least, there should be no bad bottles.

Two qualifications are needed, though, before beginning the discussion. The first is that vintage port needs an average of 15 years to reach full maturity, and no vintage can be truly assessed until the wines are mature. Comments on young vintages, then, are provisional.

The second qualification derives from the fact that vintage port divides tasters more than most wines. Perhaps this is inevitable, given that various sorts of excellence are on offer, rather than the good and the mediocre or bad. In the end it is a matter of taste as to whether you prefer the 1985s to the 1983s, or whether you prefer Warre to Graham in the latter year. Wine merchants' or writers' imperatives should be viewed with more than usual suspicion in the case of port. Try as much as possible. Nearly every bottle of port has something different to offer: that is the delight of the wine.

*M*UCH HARD work is over; much is still to come. It will be at least two years before the wine from these grapes can be called vintage port – if its quality merits.

1985

A cold January was followed by a wet February and March, and these rains were much welcomed by growers. From June onwards, weather conditions were near-perfect, with clear skies, high summer temperatures and a little rain in early September. The grapes were harvested in a very healthy condition, and the new port was notable for its early acquisition of fruit aroma and its striking blue–purple colour.

1985 was a 'universal' vintage: one declared by all shippers, and the first of this kind since 1963. An almost unanimous view is that it is the best vintage since 1977, while not possessing the depth and tannin to match that year. Comparisons are drawn with 1966. What is certain is that no vintage port has ever opened at so high a price. This is due to three factors: rapidly increasing production costs in Portugal; the growth of *en primeur* or 'pre-arrival' buying (see page 80); and unprecedented interest from America, where vintage port has finally become fashionable. The high prices are strange in the light of one factor – it is the fourth declared vintage in only six years. The market in 1987 is obviously hungry. Whether the wines justify the early confidence of their price tags remains to be seen.

At this stage they are distinguished by the rich, mouthfilling qualities that mark long-lasting vintages in early youth, and by seductive fruit flavours (blackberry, cherry, plum and loganberry appear and reappear on tasting cards). Warre, Dow, Graham and Fonseca have all been highly praised in early tastings, with Graham particularly hard to resist; Taylor, for once, seems a little overshadowed by its peers, although it has undoubtedly made a fine wine. Perhaps it will exert its authority in time. Among the Portuguese producers, Cálem has made an excellent wine.

1983

A dry winter, a wet flowering period and a cooler-than-usual summer did not suggest that a vintage year was in the offing. Magnificent weather in September altered the picture completely, and the fruit was in excellent condition when the late harvest came in.

Sixteen major shippers declared the vintage, and nearly all of those who did not had declared the previous year: 1982 and 1983 are therefore 'split' vintages. There seems little doubt that this is the better of the two, and a few critics go so far as to rate it above the 1985 vintage. The matter will not be settled until at least the end of the century, as they are both vintages that will require long maturation.

Roundness, fullness and lusciousness are the characteristics of the best wines of the year at this stage. Fonseca, Dow, Cálem, Gould Campbell and Smith Woodhouse are all proving good, while Cockburn and Quarles Harris both seem to have produced better 1983 wines than 1985s.

1982

A dry winter was followed by a very hot summer, and these near-drought conditions meant an early harvest. Eleven major shippers declared this year, led by Croft, Noval and Sandeman.

'Elegant' is a word much favoured in discussions of the wines of 1982, and its use with respect to young vintage port generally means that the wines tend towards lightness. The best are indeed elegant, soft and winsome, but it is not a consistent vintage, and there are some wines that barely merit their

YOUNG VINES on Cockburn's Vilariça development learn how to cope with the hot dry summers of the high Douro – by spreading their roots deeply into the loose schist.

vintage status, being slight and badly balanced. Noval, Ferreira, Offley Boa Vista, Ramos–Pinto and Montez Champalimaud's Quinta do Côtto are among the best, with the last named looking at this stage perhaps the finest of all, with good potential for ageing. It was a year that suited the Portuguese style of port-making – with the emphasis on accessibility and voluptuous fruit – rather than the British, who prefer tannic impenetrability in the early years. Cristiano van Zeller of Noval considers it to be "a fabulous year."

1980

A cold winter was followed by a wet, late spring, and poor flowering meant a reduced crop. After more rain in June, very hot weather began, and this continued until the harvest in September. The vintage was generally declared, although Cockburn,

Noval, Croft and Delaforce were all among the abstainers. It was a comparatively small crop.

This is another medium-quality vintage, rather like 1982, except that the slightly higher tannin levels in the wines suggest more stamina for long-term maturing. The wines are nevertheless supple and fragrant. Graham, Taylor, Rebello Valente and Gould Campbell have all made good vintage port.

1977

This year began cold and wet, and remained cold throughout much of the spring, retarding grape formation and development. The summer was comparatively cool, too, until September – when it suddenly became very, very hot. Heavy rain began on October 10th, catching out some of the later-picking farmers.

Not ideal conditions, one might think, and yet this vintage has been praised unreservedly from its declaration (by 22 shippers) onwards. The wines have sweetness, tannin and concentration: the raw ingredients of a great vintage. Comparisons are drawn with 1963. It is a vintage for long maturation: the 1977s should be at their peak around the turn of the century.

That is if everything goes as forecast. It should not be forgotten, though, that Noval and Cockburn/Martinez saw fit not to declare; and one or two of the early leaders, like Dow, have recently been tasting less aggressive than expected. Paul Symington of Dow feels that the shippers and press may have exaggerated the early promise of the 1977s. Only time will tell. The high prices of this vintage's wines indicate continuing high expectations. Taylor is considered to have made the wine of the year, while nearly every declaring shipper has produced a port of interest.

1975

A hot, dry summer followed a wet winter. There was rain again in September and just before harvesting began in October, diluting the crop somewhat.

The shippers badly needed a vintage to declare, having had nothing on their books since 1970 (Dow and Offley excepted: they offered 1972). So the vintage was generally declared. Some critics have subsequently questioned the wisdom of this, claiming that the wines are too light to deserve their vintage labels. They are light, but many have character. The vintage has certainly proved a useful one, providing ports at a reasonable price for drinking in the early and mid-1980s, while waiting for 1970 to show at its best. Fonseca produced a much-admired wine, while Delaforce and Graham are both good.

1970

The weather during this year was perfect: rain in January and February, a cold dry March, a warm April followed by a warm spring and a hot summer, then a little rain to refresh the grapes in September before a dry – though hot – harvest period.

*G*RAHAM'S CELLARS have the look of a bank vault: order, severity, and almost limitless reserves combine to tease the collector's imagination.

Originally this was considered to be an attractive, softish sort of vintage for the medium-term. In fact it is proving to be a late maturer and is still in 'hibernation'. The wines are expected to wake from their slumbers about 1990. It may then prove a finer vintage than originally anticipated: rich, well-balanced port with fragrance and complex, fresh flavour. Taylor, Fonseca, Croft, Graham and Warre are all very good, but so are others.

1966

Drought conditions throughout 1966 resulted in a small crop of rather wizened grapes. Their sugar content, though, was extremely high. The wines seemed rather coarse at first, but time has smoothed their edges: this is another vintage whose reputation has risen steadily with every passing year. The vintage is now a prized and expensive one, and is still improving. Graham is again one of the best.

Mention should also be made of **1967**, declared by only seven shippers, but those seven included Cockburn, Sandeman and Taylor. The light wines of this year are all now ready.

1963

Wet, cool spring weather was followed by a fine, dry summer; as with many of the best Douro vintages, a little rain fell before the harvest to soften the skins of the grapes and freshen their juice.

This was a Great Year. Power and aggression are still much in evidence in the wines, 25 years on. Concentration and balance have also distinguished the wines from the start, while elegance and liquorousness are now beginning to emerge from beneath the veil of tannin. Any wine from this year is well worth trying, should you be given the chance.

1960

An accessible vintage of moderate quality.

1958

A pleasant vintage but no more. Remaining wines should be drunk soon.

1955

A good vintage producing powerful wines, the very best of which are still improving.

1948

A ferociously hot summer burnt the grapes on the vines, and some wines taste pleasantly roasted. A powerful, luscious, long-lasting vintage.

1945

A magnificent vintage. All wines are still very fine, and unlikely to decline for many years.

Previous vintages of excellence: *1935, 1931, 1927, 1912, 1908, 1904*.

There will, probably, be about five great vintages in the 20th century. To date *1912, 1945* and *1963* qualify for most shippers. Does *1977*? And will there be another?

*G*RAHAM'S *1945 vintage: about £145 ($264) per bottle at London auction prices in 1988. This year saw an excellent vintage for many shippers.*

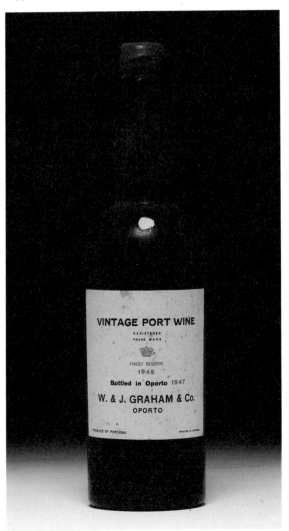

VINTAGE PORT WINE

REGISTERED
TRADE MARK

FINEST RESERVE
1945

Bottled in Oporto 1947

W. & J. GRAHAM & Co.
OPORTO

PRODUCE OF PORTUGAL

Ports from other countries

Port – or Porto – comes from Portugal. It is a fortified wine made from named grape varieties grown in a demarcated area at the far end of Western Europe. But 'port' is also a method, a way of making wines. A clear analogy can be drawn with Champagne, which comes only from the Champagne region in France – though *méthode champenoise* wines can come from anywhere in the world. Ports from other countries are not imitations of the 'original and best', but port-method wines. Some of them are of an excellence distinctly their own, so different from port that no Sandeman, Delaforce or Graham need feel his or her livelihood even remotely threatened by their existence.

There are three main countries which produce port-method wines: the USA, Australia and South Africa. Of the three, the Australians have the longest tradition of making port-method wines, and consequently theirs are, as a rule, the best. Over the last decade, a small number of specialist Californian producers have also begun to produce port-method wines of exceptional quality; while tradition, the Tinta Barroca grape and favourable climate combine to produce a small number of fine vintage port-method wines in South Africa.

Australian ports

Australian port is one of a trio of colossal dessert wines, the other two being Liqueur Muscat and Liqueur Tokay. Port is generally the lightest of the three, though 'light' is a strictly relative term in this company. The two main types of port produced are 'vintage' and 'tawny', the former being a young dated wine, and the latter an older, blended and branded (though sometimes also dated) wine. The main port-producing areas of Australia are situated along the Murray and Murrumbridgee Rivers, in the states of South Australia, New South Wales and Victoria. The most important grape varieties used are Shiraz and Grenache, with Cabernet Sauvignon, Mataro, Carignane and even Muscat also being used. Australian tawny ports are perhaps better than vintage versions, for the simple reason that in many cases more care goes into their elaboration, maturation and marketing – as 'liqueur' ports. They are often very thick and rich with a burnt, woody character, but undeniably luscious and intense. Names to look out for include Seppelt's Mount Rufus, Para 102 and dated Para ports; Penfold's Grandfather, Reynella's John Reynell; Yalumba's Galway Pipe and other limited edition ports, and

ports from Hardy and Lindeman. Vintage ports are made in a similar way, from the same pool of grape varieties, and are bottled between one year and 18 months after the vintage. All of the mentioned producers, as well as Stanton & Killeen and Brown Brothers, offer impressive examples of this otherwise rather lighter style.

American ports

Port-method wines in the United States are produced in enormous quantities, with annual production certainly dwarfing that of Portugal. American port has, though, always suffered from a poor market image, the result of faithful support from customers for whom low pricing overrides all other considerations, the nation's winos.

As one might expect, California's fine winemakers have not been content to leave things thus. California's potential for wine production is similar to that of Europe as a whole, so there should certainly be areas of the State where conditions are perfect for the production of port-method wines. A select band of producers have attempted to find those conditions.

Leaders among these are Christian Brothers, Ficklin Vineyards, J. W. Morris Wines, Quady Winery and Woodbury Winery, all of whom have made a speciality of port – Ficklin, Quady and Woodbury exclusively so. Many other wine companies, particularly the big producers such as E. and J. Gallo, include ports among their range, often

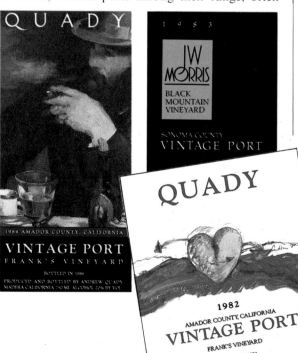

priced at a couple of dollars a bottle and tasting dull at best. This, paradoxically, makes life more difficult for the specialists than competitively priced quality wines from the same sources would. The public has had little chance to acquire a taste for good American port.

Among the specialists, Ficklin is the only company working exclusively with Portuguese grape varieties (Sousão, Tinto Cão, Touriga and Tinta Madeira – although the last two would be known by different names in Portugal). This San Joaquin winery has been in operation since 1948, and early vintages of its Ficklin Tinta Port continue to hold well in bottle. Despite the Portuguese grape varieties, this is very much a Californian dessert wine, with its rich and raisiny character.

Andrew Quady founded his winery in 1975, and made all his ports from Zinfandel until recently, when a new Amador County vineyard of Portuguese grape varieties became operational. His vintage ports are lush, rich and accessible. Russell Woodbury has been making ports since 1977 from Cabernet Sauvignon, Petite Syrah, Zinfandel and even Pinot Noir grapes in the slightly cooler area of Marin County, north of San Francisco. His ap-

A RED ROAD runs across a green vineyard on a Black Mountain. This is where Richard Mafit of J.W. Morris produces rich Sonoma County port from three varieties of old vines in California, USA.

proach is highly serious, and an interesting innovation is the use of fine pot-still brandy for fortification. The results are promising, and Woodbury's are probably the Californian vintage ports that most resemble their Old World cousins.

"I would call American Ports . . . anything but traditional," says Richard Mafit, winemaker for the J. W. Morris Winery. This company, named the J. W. Morris Port Works when operations began in 1975, is also run in a dedicated manner, producing vintage and late-bottled vintage ports from its Alexander Valley Black Mountain Vineyard, which is planted with old Zinfandel, Petite Syrah and Cabernet Sauvignon vines. J. W. Morris ports are the brawniest of those produced in California, perhaps indicating more clearly than the wines of any other producer what might be achieved in the future. Interestingly enough, despite Morris's use of non-Portuguese grape varieties, tasting notes mention chocolate and rich fruit flavours.

Californian ports are now beginning to achieve the recognition they deserve, and a 'Californian Port Producers' Guild' has been established to help educate and inform the domestic market about this still-misunderstood wine.

South African ports

Port-method wines from South Africa are produced in four main styles: ruby, tawny, vintage and white. Each corresponds approximately to its Portuguese equivalent, though the wines tend to have a soft, grapy quality rarely found in the well-known Portuguese port.

The Cape area has enormous potential for port-method wine-growing: Portuguese grape varieties (especially the Tinta Barroca) are well-established in the country, and climatic and even soil conditions are very similar in places to those of the Douro valley. There are 20 and 30 year-old South African vintage ports in existence that have realized this potential magnificently. They rarely leave South Africa, though, and are little known outside it. Leading producers include Allesverloren and KWV, the State cooperative.

Australian, American and South African port-method wines are, in general, rarely seen on sale abroad, which is due in large part to labelling problems. One can only hope these will be overcome, because being able to taste ports made from different grape varieties in different vineyards from those of Portugal is in every wine-lover's interest.

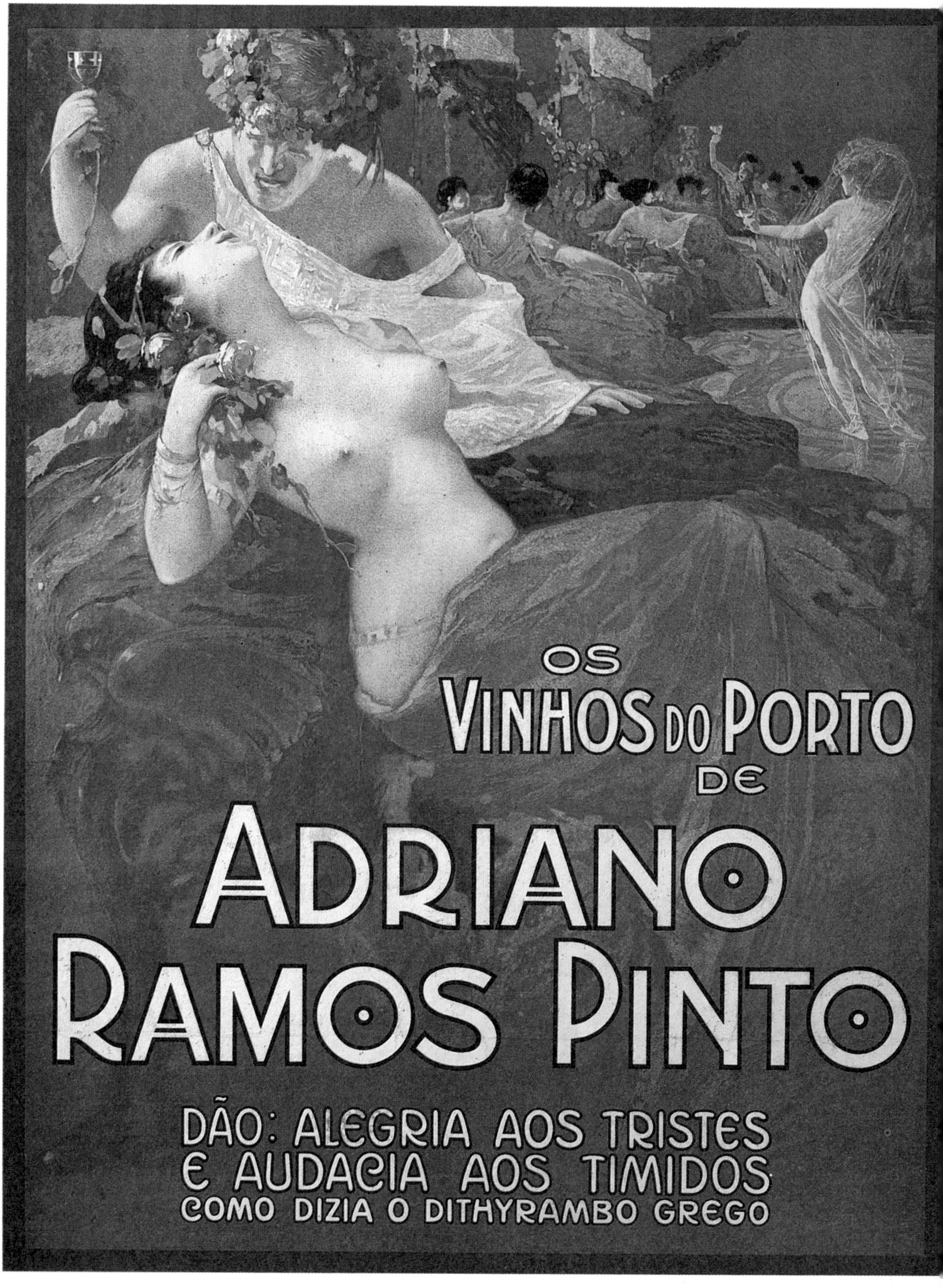

OS
VINHOS DO PORTO
DE
ADRIANO
RAMOS PINTO

DÃO: ALEGRIA AOS TRISTES
E AUDACIA AOS TIMIDOS
COMO DIZIA O DITHYRAMBO GREGO

PART THREE

The Enjoyment of Port

No words written in a book can directly affect your enjoyment of port. That is a matter for your senses and the wine itself.

What this Part of the book aims to do is provide advice on everything that might indirectly affect your enjoyment of port. Is your local supermarket the best place to buy vintage port? Is it advisable to age port in kitchen cupboards? Does popcorn make a good accompaniment to fine old tawny?

Strictly speaking, the purchase and storage of port are preliminary to its enjoyment. There are few wine enthusiasts, though, who do not enjoy buying wine and finding somewhere at home to store it: the squirrel instinct, no doubt. These activities may therefore be considered as stages one and two in the enjoyment of port.

There are many options open to the port-purchaser as to where to buy wine today. As we will see in a moment, no one outlet is right for every port purchase. We will examine the claims of each shop type in turn, beginning with what is generally the most attractive in terms of price: the supermarket.

Supermarkets are good places to buy well-known brands of port. They offer two unrivalled advantages: low price and high turnover. Ruby and tawny ports are wines blended from many sources, sold ready for drinking, and a fresh bottle will be more attractive than one that has been standing upright on a shelf for a year or more.

Port, though, may not necessarily be well cared for in a supermarket. For this reason, you should exercise caution about buying fine ports there, and particularly sediment-forming ports such as vintage, quinta or crusting ports. If you know the consignment has recently arrived and is competitively priced, then make the most of the golden opportunity. If not, consider the purchase with some circumspection.

"Any time not spent drinking port is a waste of time."
Percy Croft

There are many types of specialist wine shop, and these are in principle the best places to buy the finer qualities of port. Old vintages, in particular, should only be bought from a merchant of impeccable reputation – ideally one who has aged the wine in his own cellars. You will pay a great deal of money for a bottle of Taylor 1963, and it is important to know that it has been matured correctly. A number of old-established merchants will even decant the wine for you. This can be an extremely useful service if you wish to drink it immediately, for transporting the wine home in its bottle would almost certainly disturb the sediment to such an extent that successful decanting would be impossible for a month or so. For this level of service, you should not expect the lowest prices.

The most exciting developments in wine selling recently have been wine shops or warehouses that offer a wide range of high-quality wines at prices competitive with those of supermarkets. These are the places to go to search out young quality ports for maturing yourself, fine tawnies, and ports from less well-known shippers. The staff are usually knowledgeable, enthusiastic and informal. You can generally taste before you buy.

Port from the armchair

If you live in a remote part of the country, or prefer to buy port from home, you will have to rely on mail-order wine merchants. Many of these are old-established local merchants, who have expanded their businesses with mail-order sales. They generally offer an excellent service. Prices are not low, but the range of ports listed is often good. Do be sure, though, to give the port plenty of time to 'rest' after you take delivery, particularly in the case of bottle-aged ports. Even tawnies will not taste at their best after a long journey, and fine port of any sort should be allowed to rest and recuperate for at least a month before being opened.

The two final port-purchasing possibilities are *en primeur* or pre-arrival and auction. Except for the very old or rare bottles that regularly go under the auction hammer, you will in both these cases be buying no less than a case (12 bottles) of port, and it will almost certainly be vintage port. Considerable financial outlay is required. You should, therefore, be certain that you will enjoy what you have purchased. (Unless of course you are buying for investment, in which case you should buy the best that you can as cheaply as possible, and keep it for as long as possible in conditions of certifiable excellence.)

En primeur or pre-arrival buying means that you purchase a case or more of young vintage port when the wine is first offered for sale to the public, while it is still in Portugal. You will later have to pay transport costs, customs duty and taxes on it, but even including these costs this should be the lowest price the port will ever be offered you at. That is the

*T*HE *17TH-century cellars at Berry Bros. & Rudd Ltd – one of London's most respected wine merchants.*

theory. In practice the system has become so popular in recent years, and production costs have risen so fast in Portugal, that increasingly high prices have been asked and obtained for each new vintage, regardless of quality, often making the previous one seem better value for a few years and possibly longer. So you should think carefully before committing yourself to a purchase of this sort. If you are sure that the vintage on offer is one you want, and that the merchant you are buying from is offering the best prices (they can vary considerably), go ahead. Plan for the transport and

other costs, and make preparations to have the wine properly stored if you do not have your own cellar. Then wait twelve or fifteen years for your bargain to mature.

The alternative for the impatient is to buy mature port at auction. The hazards are different: you do not necessarily know what conditions the port has been stored under (though you will generally have a chance to taste the wine before the sale begins), and the price is the highest anyone is willing to pay. For this reason it is as well to set yourself a limit before the sale begins – and remember a buyer's premium (usually ten per cent of the hammer price) will be added afterwards, as will purchase taxes (15 per cent VAT in Britain). Port is a favourite auction wine, thanks to its robustness, reliability and longevity, so snips are rare; but wines from the less well-known shippers and unfashionable years can often be good value.

The port cellar

These, then, are the sources of port. But what do you buy? How do you set about building a port cellar?

The function of a port collection is to provide you with a bottle to drink, at peak condition, at any time. If you only want to drink vintage port, then you should acquire as much of it, old and young, as you can. Few people, though, only want to drink vintage port, so in the majority of cases an assortment is the ideal, with perhaps two or three bottles of every type that you enjoy in stock. All the same, it is better to have rather more vintage port in stock than other ports, because it is cheaper to buy it young, and availability is limited. Aim for a mixture of years: if all the vintage port in your cellar is 1977 and 1985, then there will be nothing much to drink before the next century. Some 1975, 1980 and 1982 will prove useful.

Crusting, quinta and the better tawny ports should all be included in a balanced port cellar, and if you come across rarities in this area (such as old dated or *garrafeira* ports) you should buy them when you have the chance. Up to a year's wait before drinking will harm none of these wines, and of course some crusting and single quinta ports will need at least this length of time to mature fully. Buy any 'traditional' late-bottled vintage (i.e. four-year bottlings) that you come across; and if you have enjoyed a particular late-bottled vintage of any sort, it's worth storing a few bottles for a year or two, as the same shipper's next LBV year may not be

equally to your taste. Undated ports should be bought more or less as required, holding one or two bottles of each in stock.

A quiet corner

The port cellar described above is based on the supposition that you have somewhere to store your wine. Ideally this will indeed be a cellar, and it will be as deep, dark and cool as possible. But if you do not have somewhere of this sort, there are several other options to consider.

The conditions needed to mature port properly are the same as for any other wine: darkness, stillness (lack of vibration or jolting) and a steady temperature. This should be as near 9°C (48°F) as possible, but steadiness is paramount: better a constant temperature of 16°C (62°F) than one that fluctuates frequently between 7°C (44°F) and 12°C (54°F). (Seasonal fluctuations are not a cause for concern, provided the transition from winter to summer temperatures is slow: no more than half a degree a day.)

There are, quite possibly, a number of places in your home suitable for storing and maturing port. Begin by considering corners and cupboards that are both low and central in the house: low, because heat rises, and temperature variation is therefore greater the higher up you go; and central, because day-to-day external temperatures can change by five degrees or more, so the further the wine is from the outside walls the better. If you cannot find anywhere like this, begin to consider other areas, bearing all of the above points in mind. Keep port away from its enemies: the sun, central heating radiators or boilers, cooking equipment, children, human feet in general, and vibrating machinery of any sort.

It should not be forgotten that port is a robust wine, better able than most to withstand the vicissitudes of improvised cellaring. Storage areas that would be wholly unsuitable for fine German wines or white burgundy may just pass muster for port. And if all else fails, and you are serious enough or rich enough to persist in an attempt to store and mature your own port, then there are a number of temperature-controlled wine cabinets on sale that provide perfect storage conditions. You might even consider having a spiral cellar installed beneath your home.

Tasting port

Imagine, then, that you have your cellar stocked with a variety of ports, including bottles from most of the declared vintages of the 1970s and 1980s. It is now December 1999, and celebrations are called for. Only the best will do. How do you go about tasting, serving and enjoying your port to the full?

Different types of port require different approaches. What is always the same, though, is the act of tasting, so we will begin by discussing how best to do this.

Wine appeals to three senses. Its colour attracts our eye; its aroma pleases our sense of smell; and it

CRISTIANO VAN Zeller of Quinta do Noval smells two young ports. A large copita concentrates aroma; swirling the wine in the glass helps release as much aroma from the wine as possible.

tastes good. Taste is generally considered the most important element, but to truly 'taste' wine you must take the other two components into account, too. To do this you need clear, light, clean air and a plain glass, ideally tulip-shaped. Fill the glass no more than a third full and hold it tilted through about 45 degrees, against a white background: a piece of card, a handkerchief, a table cloth. You will then not only be able to appreciate the colour of the wine, but also to gauge its development to some extent. A young vintage port, for example, will be a deep, opaque blackberry–purple at the centre, graduating to a lighter but still distinctly purple colour at the meniscus, or contact point between the wine and the glass. When it is ready to drink, 20 years later, the opacity will have gone and the wine will be clear and bright, while the colour will have changed to a warm tile red, fading to orange–brown at the rim. The more brown or brick-brown there is in the wine, the older it will be – though not necessarily in years, as a vintage of moderate quality will age far more quickly than a fine vintage.

Other ports, others colours: ruby, for example, should be as its name indicates, without a purple or brown component; while tawny will often surprise, being rather redder than its name suggests, though very light and clear. Amber-orange or rose-orange are hues often found in tawny. A tawny tawny is something of a rarity, except among the 30 or over 40 years old categories. White port varies from a medium waxy yellow to a very pale orange or yellow–pink.

All port, though, should look bright and attractive, inviting you, as it were, to carry your relationship with the wine further. If the wine lacks intensity of colour, or looks dull, this may indicate that it has been indifferently treated, and its aroma and taste are unlikely to please you.

The next stage in the tasting process is to gauge the wine's smell. Swirl the wine in the glass. (This is why it should be no more than a third full: if overfilled, you may now have port all over your jumper.) How much aroma is there, and what does this aroma remind you of?

In principle, the more aroma there is, the better: certainly all good mature vintage port should be powerfully aromatic. Immature vintage port, by contrast, sometimes goes through a phase when it loses its aroma altogether. Unlike many great wines, vintage port is characterized by no single key smell-association. Rather the opposite: there are so many components in its aroma, suggesting so many different smells, that this variety itself is almost its hallmark. There are fruit scents, particularly cherries, damsons, loganberries, plums, blackberries and blackcurrants – even melon rind. Another common scent is of dried tea leaves: the smell you experience as you open a packet of tea or a tea caddy. This smell is characteristic of the Touriga Nacional grape, and its presence indicates a substantial proportion of Touriga Nacional in the wine. Mint, chocolate, smoke, violets, sawdust, freshly mown hay, eucalyptus and camphor, roast meat, camomile, barleysugar: it may seem fanciful to suggest that there are all these scents in port, and yet they all suggest themselves repeatedly to tasters. Very old and very young port can often smell 'spirity': the port has yet to marry, or is falling apart, and the smell of brandy becomes apparent. The puzzling word 'peppery' also recurs repeatedly. Michael Broadbent defines it as 'a sort of raw harshness,' though it can also mean a pleasant spicy vigour. It, too, is common in young port, and suggests a degree of immaturity.

This gamut of smells is unlikely to be encountered in one wine, and most of them will in practice be found in vintage, single quinta and crusted wines, with some making an appearance in the better LBVs. Basic ruby, tawny and white port, and much vintage character port smells simply of port: vaguely

*I*N *VICTORIAN Britain, port was a man's drink, often enjoyed at table with cigars after the ladies had retired to another room. This 1886 drawing captures the atmosphere of such occasions: studied male informality, talk of business or politics, smoky air. The port was probably taken for granted – a lubricant of opinion rather than a presence in its own right.*

warm, vaguely rich. It is very difficult to sustain particular aromas in wines blended from many sources. This may improve in the future as new estates with simplified plantings contribute a greater proportion of wines.

Fine tawny, too, can be aromatically vague. At its best, it will have a nutty scent, specifically brazil, hazel or cobnuts: the creamier class of nut. Grapiness, smokiness, freshness (a sort of washday smell), barleysugar, a touch of liquorice: all of these may be detected from time to time in a fine tawny. But it can also simply smell sweet and mellow.

Smell forms an important part of the appreciation of taste itself. The fact is not widely understood, though it has always been a tenet of the thinking gastronome. "I am tempted to believe that smell and taste are in fact but a single composite sense, whose laboratory is the mouth and its chimney the nose," wrote Brillat-Savarin in 1825. An experiment recommended recently by the wine writer Oz Clarke, to convince oneself of this, is comparison between a mouthful of wine sipped with the nostrils pinched shut and one sipped normally. (Better still catch a cold.) The wine is 'tasted' in both instances, but all its nuance and depth of flavour disappears when the nose is blocked.

It should come as no surprise, then, to find that most of the frequently encountered tastes of port have already been mentioned as scents or smells. All of the fruit range mentioned above are tasted in port, particularly vintage port; so too are mint, chocolate, violets, roast meat and pepperiness. The tannin content of a wine not yet fully mature emerges on the tongue as 'grip' – that roughness familiar to anyone who has ever sipped very strong black tea. In addition, the wine's weight and presence on the tongue will convey other information: how concentrated the port is, how much structure it has, whether it is a big wine or an elegant wine, how the balance between sweetness and acidity and extract is resolved. A large sip is all that is required, but make sure that you take it around every area of the mouth, aerating it slightly as you do so, before swallowing. Even then, you should continue to concentrate: the wine's finish (or aftertaste, if you prefer) is an important quality factor.

Vintage ports are undoubtedly the most rewarding ports to taste, yet circumstances usually mean that they are enjoyed in company with others, after a festive or celebratory meal (and several bottles of wine). This is not the ideal moment to analyze the wine or commit its taste to memory. If you can find time before your guests arrive to make a few notes on the port, divided into colour, smell and taste categories, it will serve you well: you will have appreciated the wine fully and will remember it better afterwards, aided by your notes; and you will have a point of comparison when you come to taste your next vintage port. A good time to do this would be about an hour or so after decanting.

Decanting port

Something of a mystique surrounds the decanting process. This mystique is mystification: pouring wine off its sediment is a simple operation, requiring no more than a jug and a steady hand.

Decanting is necessary for vintage, crusting and quinta ports: those that have thrown a sediment as they matured. They will have been stored lying down, splash uppermost. (The 'splash' is the dab of white paint often seen on bottles of sediment-forming port. It is put there in the lodge to indicate which way up the bottle should lie.) The first thing to be done is to stand the bottle upright for a day or two before you wish to serve its contents. This will allow any soft or loose sediment to fall to the bottom.

Port is best decanted in advance of service, and the younger the port, the further in advance. A young vintage will benefit from eight or more hour's exposure to air, while one hour will be ample for an old wine. You need no more than a jug, though a clear glass decanter will show the wine at its best. A candle is useful, as is a funnel containing a small piece of clean muslin.

Remove the capsule from the bottle and draw the cork. Vintage port corks are long, and so the corkscrew should be. You will find the cork is stamped with the shipper's name and the vintage date. Clean the rim of the bottle thoroughly.

Now light the candle. This will be used to illuminate the sediment as it nears the bottle neck. Very dark glass is used for port bottles, so if you have no light source underneath the bottle as you pour, you will just have to stop immediately on sight of sediment in the wine leaving the bottle.

If you have a funnel and muslin, position these in the jug or decanter, then begin pouring the port from the bottle into the new container, above the light source. Do this as slowly and steadily as you can manage. Stop as soon as you catch sight of the sediment about to enter the bottle neck or decanter. The port is now ready to serve.

Various pieces of apparatus are available to

THE DECANTING process: port is poured from bottle to decanter, with the neck of the bottle over a candle or other light source. The candle illuminates the sediment inside the bottle. When it reaches the bottle neck, stop decanting.

complicate this simple affair. Port tongs are the most spectacular, but are really only of use if you think you may have trouble extracting the cork. Heat them red-hot then clamp them around the bottle neck, underneath the cork. Allow the tongs to cool for a minute or so before removing them. The top of the bottle should then snap off cleanly (use a wet cloth rather than your bare hands). You will still have to decant the wine, of course.

A decanting cradle is a delightful object. The bottle nestles in a metal harness. You turn a little handle and the cradle's screw mechanism slowly upends the bottle, allowing the port to drain gently into the decanter. Decanting cradles are generally antiques or reproduction antiques and hence expensive as well as inessential. They are, though, fun.

The best glassware to enjoy port from is thin and uncut. A simple decanter and a set of tulip-shaped glasses or large sherry copitas is ideal. Port is the most handsome of wines in plain, bright glass, and the tulip shape will help you to appreciate every dimension of the wine's colour, smell and taste.

When you serve port is very much your own affair. Vintage, vintage family and ruby ports are usually served at the end of the meal, and are so much enjoyed then that it seems churlish to suggest anything else. But palates may be jaded after a large meal. Tasting fine vintage port before a meal, or before or after lunch, or indeed at any other time of the day, can be a revelation.

Tawny port can also be served at any time, and most tawny – even fine tawny – is excellent served chilled during the summer months. (This is not blasphemous: the shippers drink it this way.) White port should always be served chilled, and makes a fine long drink in combination with tonic or soda water, and a twist of lemon peel.

It is customary to 'pass port', whether decanted or not, to the left around a table, and not to smoke until everyone present has enjoyed at least one glass. Cigars and port are a popular combination, but in truth both are best enjoyed completely on their own. Burning tobacco tyrannizes wine – and non-smoking winedrinkers.

Port and food

Port, like all dessert wines, requires no food accompaniment. Being sweet, it seems to act on the stomach as a food itself, satisfying appetite to a more marked degree than it quenches thirst or cuts heavy food. Indeed a glass of port taken as a *digestif*, in place of dessert, is as sound and sane a way of enjoying this wine as any. The lighter styles of port are equally good taken as apéritifs. Both can be perfectly appreciated in isolation.

At the opposite extreme, it is possible to drink port throughout a meal. I have done this on a number of occasions, when no other wine was available, on the principle that any wine is better than none as a lubricant and vivifier of food. The results have been satisfactory, but only that. No rule forbids the consumption of port throughout a meal, but the simple fact is that most cooked savoury dishes are not enhanced in any way by a glass of port. Its sweetness is too intrusive. Compare this with the manner in which good red wine improves the dishes it partners – which in turn improve the wine – and it becomes obvious that port's place is at either end of a meal, rather than during it.

All wine, though, is best appreciated when the palate has something else to engage its attention between sips, and port is no exception. White and tawny port enjoyed as an apéritif, for example, is served with salted almonds in Portugal, and the combination is an excellent one. Salted pistachios and cashews make a good substitute for almonds, as do baby pretzels. Freshly popped popcorn, buttered and salted, is as good as it is unorthodox. The more bizarrely flavoured snack foods, on the other hand, are best avoided. So are Japanese rice crackers: their sweet malty taste and seaweed seasoning – so good with a dry apéritif – disagree with port.

In colder climates, of course, most port is consumed at room temperature after meals, and often with the cheese course. Port and Stilton, in particular, make a hallowed combination, and great temerity is needed to question it. I question it. The necessarily acrid flavour of Stilton veining, particularly in vigorous farmhouse examples, is the reason: this is a flavour that can be enjoyed on its own, or

PORT AND Stilton is a popular combination in Britain, especially at Christmas. Port certainly flatters Stilton; whether Stilton returns the compliment is less certain. Fresh nuts and plain cheeses form the best partnerships with fine port, permitting full appreciation of the wine's nuances. Apples will find out a port's faults, if any – hence the merchant's adage "Buy on apples; sell on cheese". Grapes make a refreshing and appropriate combination with port.

tempered by a dry biscuit, but it does nothing for fine port except run amok with its balance and distort its fruit. Stilton if you must, but choose a mild and creamy example, or a white Stilton.

Irrigating a large Stilton with port is a popular British Christmas pastime. This is harmless and diverting, and the sweetness of the wine gives the cheese an intriguing edge. Whether it would improve a fine Stilton in any way is questionable, and the port used should be no better than a simple ruby. The best method of ingress for the wine is via a series of narrow skewered holes. Pouring a glass of port into the centre of a scooped-out cheese is less satisfactory, producing, in Ambrose Heath's words, "a purplish kind of mash of cheese and wine of the most disgusting smell and appearance."

Other cheeses make superb partners for port, particularly the plainer and harder varieties. Farmhouse Cheddar and Cheshire, and the Scottish Dunlop, are all ideal with port. Just as the neutral brandy provides a canvas for the excitement and colour of the half-fermented wine, so the slightly nutty flavours of these cheeses makes a perfect canvas for the rich fruit of mature port. Swiss cheeses such as Emmenthal, Gruyère or Tête de Moine also combine memorably with port; as does fine whole Parmesan, Very Old Gouda or Spanish Manchego. This is a field where experiment is worthwhile, and some unexpected combinations can be surprisingly good. It is only strong blue cheeses that are best avoided.

Nuts and sweet fruits

Nuts are as good with port at the dessert stage as they are before a meal. Walnuts, brazils, almonds and fresh, milky cobnuts are all superb between sips of port: they are rich with a distinct yet mild flavouring, and this is the gastronomic partnership that port, in its flamboyance, seeks.

Sweet fruits are sometimes eaten with port – Taylor, for example, has recently taken to advertising its LBV beside a cut fig. You might also like to try peaches, apricots, nectarines and ripe pears with port, in addition to fruit-based desserts. Such combinations are either to your taste or not: fruit can certainly alter the taste of the wine (whereas nuts or mild cheese simply enhance it) but you may enjoy the altered taste, particularly if you are fond of fruit. Desserts always have the effect of making port taste dryer – but this in itself can reveal the wine in an intriguing new light.

*P*ORT CAN *be enjoyed at any time of day (above). Its tonic virtues are most evident mid-morning and late afternoon.*

This 1905 Strand illustration (below) shows the men lingering exclusively over their port well into Edwardian times. Cigar smoke continues to eclipse the wine's aroma.

P A R T   F O U R

Epilogue

This book began with a brief examination of what the word 'port' suggests: a fortified dessert wine, seas and seafaring, a harbour, a homecoming. We then passed to more specific examination of the first of these meanings and connotations, and our attention has barely wandered since. By way of an Epilogue, perhaps we might drift into a peopled reverie. When we sit and enjoy a glass of port, who enjoys it – in imagination, at least – with us?

There are the people we know about, and there are the people we do not know about. We know about Dr Johnson and Swift, but they were by no means the only writers to enjoy port. Tennyson, of course, relished his 'pint of port' – when authentic:

> Go fetch a pint of port:
>   But let it not be such as that
> You set before chance-comers,
>   But such whose father-grape grew fat
> On Lusitanian summers.

Keats enjoyed port, as he did all wines, rapturously: "I pitched upon another bottle of claret – Port – we enjoyed ourselves very much were all very witty and full of wine –"; and we might note in passing that the 'claret' so beloved by Keats, Marghanita Laski has argued, could well have been none other than red *vinho verde*.

It is Dickens, though, that we chiefly think of in connection with port. Dickens enjoyed port (there were nearly 11 dozen bottles of various vintages in his cellar at the time of his death, as well as 18 magnums of an unspecified shipper's 1851); though he enjoyed Champagne more. His books are not overfull of references to the wine. It is his world, rather – our great image of Victorian times from a writer of the heart rather than the head – that seems redolent of port, with its repeated celebrations of Christmas, of London, of hearth and home, of cheer, sympathy and generosity. Other literary Victorians wrote about port, but many were writers of the head, and failed (albeit memorably), like Meredith, in their evocation:

> Of all our venerable British of the two Isles
> professing a suckling attachment to an
> ancient port-wine, lawyer, doctor, squire,
> rosy admiral, city merchant, the classic
> scholar is he whose blood is most nuptial to
> the webbed bottle. The reason must be, that
> he is full of the old poets. He has their spirit
> to sing with, and the best that Time has
> done on earth to feed it. He may also
> perceive a resemblance in the wine to the
> studious mind, which is the obverse of our
> mortality, and throws off acids and crusty
> particles in the piling of the years until it is
> fulgent by clarity. Port hymns to his
> conservatism. It is magical: at one sip he is
> off swimming in the purple flood of the ever
> youthful antique.

PORT WAS not always denied Victorian women dinner-guests, as this cartoon of 1888 shows.

FAIR HOSTESS *(passing the wine): "I hope you admire this decanter, Admiral! . . ."*
GALLANT ADMIRAL: *"Ah – it's not the* Vessel *I'm admiring . . ."*
FAIR HOSTESS: *"I suppose it's the* Port *. . ."*
GALLANT ADMIRAL: *"Oh no: It's the* Pilot!*"*

Mighty words, but they tell us mighty little. Compare this with Dickens's *Bleak House* description of the impenetrable lawyer Tulkinghorn's after-dinner treat:

> . . . Mr Tulkinghorn sits at one of the open windows, enjoying a bottle of old port. Though a hard-grained man, close, dry, and silent, he can enjoy old wine with the best. He has a priceless bin of port in some artful cellar under the Fields, which is one of his many secrets. When he dines alone in chambers, as he has dined to-day, and has his bit of fish and his steak or chicken brought in from the coffee-house, he descends with a candle to the echoing regions below the deserted mansion, and, heralded by the remote reverberation of thundering doors, comes gravely back, encircled by an earthy atmosphere and carrying a bottle from which he pours a radiant nectar, two score and ten years old, that blushes in the glass to find itself so famous, and fills the whole room with the fragrance of southern grapes.

It is this passage, rather than the previous one, that perfectly sums up the magic and lure of old (here 50-year-old) vintage port.

But it is not only writers – and their characters – that form a ghostly society sipping port with us. There are also the winemakers and shippers themselves. The Abbot of Lamego is certainly there, with his special cask or two; as are Job Bearsley and his pioneering clan, and the vermin- and bandit-ridden Thomas Woodmass. Baron Forrester, with his maps, monographs and fateful money belt, is among the company; so too is the stubborn Mr Wright, the persistent Mr Dow, the optimistic Mr Sandeman – and Cabel Roope, a shipper famous for his appalling Portuguese. (When spending a day at the races, Mr Roope had the honour to be asked by King Carlos I whether or not he had a horse running in the next race. "Sir, teno uma cavala muito beng thought-of," came the reply. This would have been comprehensible if inelegant, save for the fact that Roope had confused the word for horse, *cavalo*, with that for mackerel, *cavala*. The king, no doubt, awaited the race with interest.) Dona Antónia Adelaide Ferreira would be there, with both husbands; as would the plucky American, Joseph Camo. Perhaps Pombal or even Wellington would take a glass; and the garrulous Bishop of Norwich, a famous 'bottle-stopper', would have his hold on the decanter closely scrutinized.

All of these people we know about, but many more, every bit as fascinating, every bit as eccentric, we have no knowledge of. All of those who enjoyed pints of port in the taverns of the 18th century, bottles of port in the coaching inns of the 19th century, and port-and-lemon in the pubs of the 1920s and 1930s – millions on millions of people – form a drinking tradition that, when we enjoy a glass of port, we too become part of. Of few other wines can this be so richly and memorably said.

Further reading

If you have found this introduction to the subject of interest, then there are four books that will each, in different ways, broaden your knowledge of port.

The Story of Port - *The Englishman's Wine*
Sarah Bradford
Christie's Wine Publications
black-and-white photographs and drawings

A scholarly account of the history of port combined with a detailed overview of the port scene in the 1970s. Scrupulously researched and attractively written, this is the best general book on the subject.

Port
George Robertson
Faber and Faber
no photographs, some black-and-white drawings

This book is a good buy for anyone interested in the technical side of port winemaking as its detail on this aspect is unrivalled. It contains no organized information, however, on shippers, and is cursory on port styles and other consumer matters. The book is written in an agreeably old-fashioned manner, and contains a fascinating personal reminiscence of a 1953 journey down the Douro in a *barco rabelo*.

Rich, Rare and Red - *A Guide to Port*
Ben Howkins
London: Christopher Helm
San Francisco: The Wine Appreciation Guild
black-and-white photographs and woodcuts

This book has the widest scope of all those discussed here, and contains useful chapters on visiting the region and on local food and wine. The author's extensive knowledge of his subject is well-served by his easy, readable style.

Port - *An Introduction to its History and Delights*
Wyndham Fletcher
Sotheby Publications
colour plates, black-and-white photographs and drawings

Despite its rather random structure, this elegantly written book is a mine of curious and entertaining information on port, and much else besides. The author's first-hand account of the London port trade (and specifically the Cockburn office) in the 1920s and 1930s is a gem: it must read – to contemporary IDV or Seagram executives – like a choice passage from Dickens. There is also some excellent technical information, including a detailed discussion of the Douro Vineyard Register.

Picture credits

Templar Publishing would like to extend their grateful thanks to all the port shippers and importers without whose help and enthusiasm this book could not have been produced. Special thanks are extended to Tim Stanley-Clarke, Dow's Port; Roberto Guedes, Forrester & Co; and Adriana Ramos-Pinto, Ramos-Pinto S.A.

Illustrations, *pages 13, 37, 41 and 81*, by Chris Forsey.
Photographic credits (*a = above, b = below, m = middle, l = left, r = right*):
Cover: Michael Little Photography
Berry Bros. & Rudd Ltd: *page 80*.
Cockburn Smithes & Co Ltd: *pages 11, 12, 13, 18, 25, 27, 29, 41b, 44l, 44r, 46l, 47r, 51a, 52l, 53, 55, 58, 73, 81*.
C. da Silva S.A.: *page 52r*.

Chambers Cox & Co Ltd/Quinta do Noval: *page 65, 87a, 88*.
Dow's Port: *pages 9, 15, 42a, 48l, 48r, 54b, 85a*.
Mary Evans Picture Library: *pages 17, 19, 35, 83b, 87b, 89*.
J.E. Fells & Sons Ltd: *pages 14, 43a, 56*.
A.A. Ferreira Ltd: *pages 36, 61*.
Forrester & Co: *pages 10, 33, 37, 39b, 54a, 92, 93*.
W & J Graham & Co: *pages 22, 23, 50, 62, 74, 75*.
I.D.V. Ltd: *page 59*.
Michael Little Photography: *page 24*.
The Mansell Collection: *pages 16a, 15, 21b*.
J.W. Morris: *page 77*.
Osborne Publicity: *page 86*.
Portuguese Government Trade Office: *pages 79, 90*.
Ramos-Pinto S.A.: *page 8, 16b, 78*.
Taylor, Fladgate & Yeatman: *pages 42b, 69*.
Warre & Co Ltd: *pages 49a, 70, 72*.
J. Wyand: *pages 21a, 32, 34, 39a, 40, 41a, 43b, 45l, 45r, 46r, 47l, 49b, 51b, 60, 68, 82, 83a*.

Index